TUNES AND WOODEN SPOONS

Mary Janet MacDonald

MacIntyre Purcell Publishing Inc.

Muffins & Loaves

Carrot Cream Cheese Muffins

1 cup white sugar
2/3 cup canola/vegetable oil
2 eggs
1 teaspoon vanilla
2 cups grated carrots
¾ teaspoon salt
1 ¼ teaspoons cinnamon
1 ¼ cups all-purpose flour
1 teaspoon baking soda

Cream Cheese Filling
1-250-gram block cream cheese
¼ cup white sugar
1 teaspoon vanilla
Pinch salt

Mix sugar, oil, eggs, vanilla together. Add grated carrots. Stir dry ingredients together and add to wet ingredients and blend well. Set aside.

Prepare the cream cheese filling by placing the cheese, sugar, vanilla and salt together in a bowl and blending together by hand or with an electric beater for about 1 minute. Set aside.

This will make 15 muffins so line muffin tins with 15 liners. Put a heaping tablespoon of batter into each muffin cup. Now put about a tablespoon of the cream cheese filling on top of the batter in each muffin cup. Flatten down the cream cheese filling a tiny bit and make sure to use all the cream cheese filling. Add another tablespoon of batter over the top of each muffin until all the batter is used up over the 15 muffins.

Bake at 350 F for about 20 minutes (but start checking after 16-17 minutes mark). Test with a cake tester but not through the middle of the muffin, instead try off to the side. Place on wire rack to cool. Muffins will sink down in the middle a little bit and that is just fine (this will happen because the cream cheese mixture is softer). These muffins are to die for.

Morning Glory Muffins

Bowl # 1 (large bowl)
2 cups all-purpose flour
1 cup sugar
2 teaspoons baking powder
½ teaspoon baking soda
2 teaspoons cinnamon
¼ teaspoon salt

Mix well and add:
2 large carrots, shredded or grated (about 2 cups)
2 medium apples shredded or grated (about 1 cup)
½ cup raisins (optional)
½ cup walnuts or pecans** (optional) See note below)
Mix well with the flour mixture.

In Bowl # 2 (small bowl)
3 eggs (whisked)
¾ cup vegetable or canola oil
2 teaspoons vanilla
Whisk all together and add all at once to flour mixture until all blended.

Scoop into a muffin tin sprayed with cooking spray (or use muffin liners). This will make about 15 muffins.

Bake at 350 F for about 23-25 minutes.

** Options: instead of adding the raisins and nuts, change it up and add ½ cup pineapple chunks or tidbits, and a ½ cup coconut. Makes for a delicious change.

Blueberry Yogurt Muffins

In a 4-cup measuring cup (or a bowl that holds 4 cups) – place the following:
2 cups vanilla yogurt
2 teaspoons baking soda
Mix together and set aside.

In large bowl place:
1 cup brown sugar
2 eggs
1 cup oil
2 teaspoons vanilla

In another bowl place:
2 cups all-purpose flour
4 teaspoons baking powder
¼ teaspoon salt

Combine yogurt mixture and flour mixture alternately to the brown sugar/eggs/oil/vanilla mixture. Then, fold in 1½ cups natural wheat bran and 1 cup fresh blueberries (or frozen).

Bake at 350 F for 22-25 minutes. Makes about 2 dozen muffins.

Banana Nut Muffins

Mix the following dry ingredients together in a bowl:
1½ cups flour
½ teaspoon cinnamon
1 teaspoon baking powder
1 teaspoon baking soda
¼ teaspoon salt

In a larger bowl mix together the following ingredients:
3 medium mashed bananas
2/3 cup white sugar
1 egg
1 teaspoon vanilla
½ cup melted butter

Mix the dry ingredients into the wet ingredients and stir until just incorporated.
Spoon the mixture into lined muffin tin (makes 12 muffins).

Next, make the topping by mixing together:
1/3 cup packed brown sugar
2 tablespoons flour
2 tablespoons butter
2 tablespoons rolled oats
½ tsp cinnamon
1/3 cup chopped pecans

Sprinkle topping over muffins.

Bake at 350 F for 20-25 minutes.

CRANBERRY ORANGE MUFFINS

Combine the following:
2 cups flour
¾ cup white sugar
1 tsp. baking powder
½ tsp. soda
½ tsp. salt
1 tsp. orange rind
1 cup frozen cranberries (cut cranberries in half and do not thaw)

In a separate bowl, combine the following:
1 egg, beaten
¾ cup orange juice
¼ cup oil

Add the liquids to the flour mixture and stir until just moistened.

Spoon the batter into muffin tins that have been prepared with cooking spray (or use muffin liners).

Bake at 400 F for 16-20 minutes.

Makes 1 dozen muffins.

Banana Loaf

¼ cup soft salted butter
1 cup white sugar
3 large ripe bananas (mashed)
2 eggs beaten well
1½ cups all-purpose flour
¼ teaspoon salt
1 teaspoon baking soda
½ cup chopped walnuts and/or ½ cup chocolate chips (optional)

Cream butter with sugar. Add mashed bananas and beaten egg. Add flour, baking soda, salt, chopped walnuts, and/or chocolate chips (as desired).

Butter or line a 9x5 inch loaf pan. If using parchment, let the edges hang over the ends. (This will make the loaf easier to remove from the pan when it is warm.) Spoon the batter into the prepared pan.

Bake at 350 F for about 1 hour and 10 minutes. Use toothpick or cake tester at the 1-hour mark and if it comes out dry – take the loaf out of the oven and set to cool.

Blueberry Orange Loaf

In large mixing bowl place:
2 cups all-purpose flour
1 teaspoon baking powder
¼ teaspoon baking soda
½ teaspoon salt

Slice an orange in half and juice it (if adding a glaze). Set the juice aside and zest the orange. Add the zest to the dry ingredients and mix well.

In a small bowl:
2 tablespoons soft salted butter
¼ cup boiling water (poured over butter)
Mix until butter is all melted.

In a small bowl mix:
1 egg
1 cup white sugar
½ cup orange juice
Add the hot water/butter mixture.

Make a well in the dry ingredients and add the egg mixture. When well blended, fold in 1 cup fresh blueberries (or if using frozen berries add about ¼ cup more).

Pour batter into a parchment lined 9x5 inch loaf pan and let the paper drape over the sides.

Bake at 350 F for about 1 hour and test with cake tester. Leave in pan for 15 minutes on cooling rack, then cool on rack until completely cool. Wrap in foil and leave overnight. Moist and delicious.

Variations:
Sugar/Orange Glaze: Prepare an orange glaze (similar to lemon loaf) by mixing up ½ cup white sugar and the juice of one orange in a small saucepan over medium heat. Cook until sugar is melted, about 1-2 minutes. Immediately pour over hot orange loaf (while it's still in the pan) and leave it to set for 15 minutes.
Remove to cooling rack until completely cooled and then wrap in foil and leave overnight. Extra moist and delicious!!

Orange Icing Glaze:
Prepare an icing glaze (similar to cinnamon rolls) by mixing up 1 tablespoon soft salted butter, 1 cup of icing sugar, and some orange juice until it becomes a thin glaze that can be poured over the loaf. After the loaf has cooled for about 5 minutes, pour the glaze over the loaf and continue letting it cool in the pan for another 10 minutes. Remove to cooling rack until completely cooled and then wrap in foil and leave overnight. Another extra moist and delicious option!!

Ethel's Pumpkin Loaf

Bowl # 1
4 eggs
2 cups sugar
1¼ cup vegetable oil
1 can pumpkin pie filling (540 ml) (Note: NOT pumpkin puree)
Beat with electric beater until well combined. Set aside.

Bowl # 2
3 cups all-purpose flour
3 teaspoons cinnamon
1 teaspoon allspice
1 teaspoon mace
2 teaspoons baking soda
2 teaspoons baking powder
½ teaspoon salt
Mix dry ingredients together. Pour into pumpkin mixture and beat with electric beater.

Optional Add-ins:
1 cup chopped walnuts
1 cup raisins
1 cup chopped pecans
Stir in optional add-ins.

Pour batter into two 9x5 inch loaf pans that have been lined with parchment paper. Feel free to sprinkle some chopped walnuts, pecans, or pumpkin seeds over the top.

Bake at 350 F for about an hour. Test with cake tester. May need 10 minutes more. Cool on cooling rack. Serve with a swipe of butter or leave as is. Delicious.

Lemon Loaf

(From the kitchen of John Allan Cameron – adapted from a recipe by Dinah Shore)

1 cup salted butter plus 2 tablespoons softened butter
3 cups white sugar
6 eggs
1½ cups milk
4½ cups all-purpose flour
1½ tablespoons baking powder
1½ teaspoons salt
Rind of 3 lemons, finely grated

If using a food processor place all ingredients (except lemon rind) together and blend well. If mixing by hand (or with an electric mixer) mix softened butter, then mix in sugar, and then eggs. Mix well. Blend in milk. Mix dry ingredients (flour, baking powder, & salt) and add to wet ingredients and blend until well mixed. Stir in lemon rind.

Pour into 3 loaf pans which have been greased or lined with parchment paper. My 2 pans are 9x5 inches (inside measurement) and the other is just a tad larger.

Bake at 350 F on center rack of oven for about one hour (or until toothpick/cake tester comes out clean). Do not overbake or the loaves will be dry! Remove immediately from pans and place on a parchment lined cookie sheet (right side up).

Glaze:
Just before the loaves are cooked, mix the lemon glaze. In a heavy saucepan, combine 1½ cups white sugar and the juice of 3 lemons and cook over medium heat for about 2 minutes or until sugar is completely dissolved. Pour the hot lemon glaze over the hot loaves. Let stand for about an hour or until completely cooled. Wrap in foil and then plastic wrap. Store in plastic container and keep on counter or in refrigerator. Best consumed in the first 3 days. Freezes well. Or even better - share with neighbours and friends.

Cookies & Squares

Chocolate Chip Jumbles

1 cup salted butter
¾ cup brown sugar
¾ cup white sugar
1 egg
1 teaspoon vanilla
1¾ cup all-purpose flour
1 teaspoon baking soda
1 teaspoon salt
¾ cup rolled oats (quick oats, minute oats)
1 bag chocolate chips (or 2 cups)

Mix all ingredients together. Drop on parchment lined cookie sheet.

Bake at 350 F for about 11 minutes (watch carefully). If the edges are brown and the middle kind of puffed up, take them out and leave on cookie sheet until they settle down. Delicious!!!

Port Hood Grandma's Crisp Molasses Cookies

¾ cup shortening
1 cup sugar
1 egg
¼ cup molasses
2 cups all-purpose flour
1 teaspoon salt
2 teaspoons baking powder
1 teaspoon each of cinnamon, cloves, and ginger

Cream shortening and add in sugar, add egg and molasses. Add flour, salt, baking powder, and spices. Mix well until combined. Roll into small balls and dip one side in some white sugar. Place sugar side up on a parchment lined cookie sheet and press down with a fork.

Bake in a 375 F oven for about 10-12 minutes. Cookies are still somewhat soft while warm but they will crisp up when cold. Great as "dunkers" in hot tea or in a cold glass of milk.

Everything that's good and tasty has so many calories in it.

Shortbread Cookies

1 cup softened salted butter – beaten
Add 1 egg yolk and 1 teaspoon vanilla and mix well.
Add:
2 cups all-purpose flour
½ cup icing sugar
Dash of salt.

Mix well using hands (or an electric beater) until flour is well incorporated. This will take a while if using a beater but it will all come together into a nice dough.

Roll out until about ¼ inch thick. When rolling the dough out, don't use flour, instead put a big piece of parchment paper on the counter – place dough on it – then place another piece of parchment paper on top. Use a favourite cookie cutter to cut out the cookies. Place on a parchment-lined cookie sheet.

Bake at 350 F for about 10-12 minutes. Watch carefully and check bottom of a cookie to test. Bottoms should be lightly browned – not dark. The tops WILL NOT be brown.

Frosting
Beat with electric beater:
¼ cup soft salted butter
1 teaspoon vanilla
3½ tablespoons milk
2¼ cups icing sugar

Put a dab on each cookie with a spoon OR better yet, use a flower/star tip decorator and garnish with cherry pieces or walnuts, or just the icing by itself. Enjoy!

Clean your doughy bowl with flour.

Grandma's Sugar Cookies

Mix the following together and set aside:
2 cups all-purpose flour
½ teaspoon salt
½ teaspoon soda
1 teaspoon cream of tartar.

Blend the following after each addition:
½ cup shortening
½ cup salted butter
1 cup white sugar
½ cup brown sugar
1 egg
1 teaspoon vanilla

Add dry ingredients and mix well until it's a big ball of dough. Form into 1-inch balls. Dip one side into white sugar and place sugar side up on cookie sheet. Press down with a fork.

Bake at 350 F for 10 minutes or so.

GINGERSNAPS

Place the following in a bowl and stir well:
¾ cup fancy molasses and fill to 1 cup with white sugar.

Add 1 cup room temperature shortening (you can microwave it a bit but do not let it melt). Mix well until you can't see any white from the shortening.

In a separate bowl place:
2½ cups flour
1 heaping teaspoon ground ginger
½ teaspoon baking soda
1 teaspoon salt

Mix in this mixture of flour a little at a time, beating well after each addition.

Here are the choices you have to prepare for the pan:

Mamie's version: As soon as the dough is mixed, form into balls (about 1 inch) and place on an UNGREASED cookie sheet (no parchment) and with the heel of your hand, flatten the cookie into a rectangle shape until quite thin. After making your first pan (the way Mamie makes them), put the remaining dough in the freezer bag and freeze until you want to make more.

Second Version: Place the dough into a parchment lined loaf pan (9 x 5 inches) and press the dough down until it is solidly in the pan. Cover with the overlap of parchment paper and place in the fridge for a couple of hours. Remove from the loaf pan and slice thinly and place on UNGREASED cookie sheet. Wrap remaining dough and place in the fridge or freezer. It will last a long time.

Stay away from cooking molasses!!! Only use Fancy molasses.

Bake cookies in a 325 F oven for 8-10 minutes. Watch carefully and watch for browning just around the edges. Let cool on cooling rack. These should be hard and snappy and are great to dunk in a glass of milk or dunked very briefly in a hot cup of tea.

Peanut Butter Chocolate Chip Cookies

½ cup salted butter or margarine
½ cup peanut butter
¼ cup white sugar
½ cup brown sugar (firmly packed)
1 egg
1¼ cups all-purpose flour
¾ teaspoon soda
¼ teaspoon salt
1 cup chocolate chips

Cream butter and peanut butter and add sugars, then add egg. In a separate bowl put the flour, soda, and salt and stir well – add to creamed mixture, then add the chocolate chips. Drop by tablespoon or scoop onto a cookie sheet lined with parchment paper.

Bake at 375 F for 10-12 minutes. If it looks like they're not quite baked in the centre at that time – best to take them out then and let them settle on the cookie sheet for about 10 minutes before removing from rack. Absolutely scrumptious!!!

Oatmeal Raisin Cookies

Stir the following together and set aside:
1½ cups all-purpose flour
1½ teaspoon baking powder
¼ teaspoon baking soda
1 teaspoon cinnamon
1 teaspoon salt
2½ cups rolled oats
1 cup raisins

In a large bowl:
1 cup soft butter or margarine (room temperature is best)
1 cup firmly packed brown sugar
¼ cup white sugar
2 eggs (room temperature is best)
1 tablespoon vanilla
1 tablespoon fancy molasses

Mix the butter, brown and white sugars together and then add the eggs, vanilla, and molasses. Add the dry ingredients and mix just until combined.

Drop by tablespoon or use a small scoop and place on parchment lined baking sheet. With the heel of your hand – press each one down a bit.

Bake at 350 F for about 10-12 minutes. Let cool 5 minutes on cooling rack and then remove from pan. These freeze really well for up to 4 months.

Fat Archie Cookies

Mix the following together and set aside:
2½ cups flour (if making drop cookies) OR
4 cups (approximately) (if rolling out)
1 teaspoon cinnamon
1 teaspoon ginger
1 teaspoon nutmeg (optional)
1 teaspoon salt

In larger bowl mix the following together until well blended:
½ cup shortening
½ cup white sugar and
½ cup brown sugar
To this mixture, add:
1 egg and mix well.
Add ½ cup molasses and mix.

Then mix together ½ cup boiling water and 2 teaspoons baking soda and add to the creamed ingredients and stir well.

Add the dry ingredients to the creamed ingredients.

If making only drop cookies, you can now drop them by teaspoons onto a parchment lined baking sheet. If rolling out, take half the batter and pat into a ball and place between 2 sheets of parchment paper and roll out to about ¼" thickness or however thick you like them. If so desired – you can sprinkle with a little white sugar or leave plain.

Bake in a 350 F oven for 10 minutes.

Replace your baking soda after a month or six weeks.

MACAROONS

2 - 200 gram bags of medium sweetened coconut (or approximately 4 cups).
¾ cup sweetened condensed milk (plus 2 table-spoons)
1 teaspoon vanilla
2 egg whites
¼ tsp. salt
Optional: 4 ounces semi-sweet chocolate (chopped)

Line 2 baking sheets with parchment paper.

Mix the coconut, milk, and vanilla and set aside.

In a deep bowl beat the egg whites and salt until stiff peaks form. Use a large spatula to fold the egg whites into the coconut mixture and set aside.

Using a small ice cream scoop or two spoons, form heaping tablespoons of the mixture into mounds on the prepared baking sheets spacing about 1-inch apart.

Bake at 325 for about 20-25 minutes - and watch carefully, rotating the pan halfway through and when the tops and edges are golden. Let cool on the pans for a few minutes and then transfer to a wire rack to cool completely.

If dipping the macaroons in chocolate, melt the chocolate in a microwave-safe bowl at medium power and stop and stir at 30 second intervals until smooth and creamy. (Or you can melt in a double boiler.) Let excess chocolate drip back into bowl and then place the macaroons back onto the parchment paper. Put pan in refrigerator for about 10 minutes. Store in airtight container. Macaroons will last about a week at room temperature.

Pork Pies

Use a tartlet pan (mini muffin tin) – tart size approximately 1½ inch tarts

Tart Shells:
1 cup salted butter
2 cups all-purpose flour
2 tablespoons icing sugar
Mix well with hands until dough is well mixed and forms a ball of dough. Take a small amount of dough and form into a ball until it measures about ¾ inch and put in each tartlet space – shaping with fingers until it forms a little 'pie crust' but not as thin as a pie crust. Alternatively, use a mini tart shaper.

Bake at 350 F for 12 minutes or until lightly browned on the edges. Remove from oven and place on rack until cool. Once completely cooled, remove each tart and place on cookie rack before adding the filling.

Filling:
2¼ cups of pitted dates, chopped
1 cup water
3/4 cup brown sugar
1 teaspoon vanilla
¼ teaspoon salt
Put all ingredients in medium sized pot and cook over medium heat until soft (6-7 minutes). Mash a little with a masher or fork to make nice and smooth. Let cool to room temperature.

Spoon the filling into each tartlet shell.

Frosting:
¼ cup soft salted butter
1 teaspoon pure maple flavouring
2 ¼ cups icing sugar
3 ½ tablespoons milk
Mix well with an electric beater until nice and smooth and put a tiny dab on each pork pie. I use a cake decorator with my favourite star tip. Only put one little dab on each tart as too much icing takes away from the date filling.

Store in plastic container and keep in refrigerator until served.

Butter Tarts

1 cup room temperature salted butter
1 egg yolk
2 cups all-purpose flour
½ cup icing sugar
Dash of salt

Prepare muffin tins by greasing lightly with butter, or cooking spray, and then a light dusting of icing sugar (or flour). Or, if you have muffin liners (especially the parchment style ones) – this might be the best choice as these shells tend to be very, very delicate, and hard to remove from the tin.

Mix the butter and egg yolk until combined. Add the flour, icing sugar and salt and either mix with your hands or use an electric beater – this may take a while, but it will all come together eventually. Form into two balls. Take one ball and roll out between 2 pieces of parchment paper that has been lightly dusted with icing sugar or flour. Roll out until about 1/8" thick. Use a 4" cookie cutter and place in a prepared muffin tin. Set aside and make filling.

Filling:
2 eggs (or 1 egg for a runnier filling)
½ cup brown sugar
½ cup maple syrup
¼ cup melted salted butter
1 teaspoon vanilla
¼ teaspoon salt

Options:
Plain with no fruit or nuts
Currants
Raisins
Pecans
Walnuts
Coconut
Chocolate Chips

Whisk the eggs, sugar, syrup, butter, vanilla and salt. If want to add one of the optional add-ins, sprinkle a few pecans or other options in the bottom of the tart shell but only in a single layer and then spoon some filling in each tart to about three-quarter full.

Bake at 425 F for about 10 minutes (or less) - check after 8 minutes. Remove from oven and cool completely on wire rack. Definitely must let these cool completely so that the filling can set. Use a fork or cake tester to leverage them out of the muffin tin.

This will make about 12 tarts.

Chocolate Coconut Balls

Mix the following together:
½ cup salted butter (melted)
¼ cup evaporated milk
1 teaspoon vanilla

Add:
3 cups coconut, (medium sweetened)
(Note: will need 2-200-gram bags in order to
have 3 cups)
2 cups icing sugar

Mix well and cover with plastic wrap and refrigerate
for at least 3 hours or overnight. Remove from fridge
and form into small balls (about 1 inch round). Return
to refrigerator for an hour.

Chocolate Coating:
In top of double boiler, melt 2 cups chocolate chips
with ¼ bar of cooking wax or 1/3 cup of cooking wax
granules. Another choice would be to add 2 tablespoons of shortening instead of the cooking wax.

Use a fork or a skewer and take a coconut ball and
using a spoon – spoon the melted chocolate over
the coconut ball and place on a parchment lined
cookie sheet. Continue in this fashion until they're
all done. Recipe makes about 40 balls.

Peanut Butter Balls

Mix together:
1 cup peanut butter
¼ cup softened salted butter

Add:
1 cup icing sugar
Mix well. And add:
2 cups crispy rice cereal and mix until well combined.

Refrigerate for 2 hours and then form into balls. Return to refrigerator for a couple of hours or overnight.

Chocolate Coating
In top of double boiler, melt 2 cups chocolate chips with ¼ bar of cooking wax or 1/3 cup cooking wax granules. Another choice would be to add 2 tablespoons of shortening instead of the cooking wax.

Use a fork or a skewer and take a ball and using a spoon – spoon the melted chocolate over the ball and place on a parchment lined cookie sheet. Continue in this fashion until they're all done. Recipe makes about 40 balls.

Bake extra and share with family, friends, and essential workers.

41

Chocolate Cookie Truffles

500-gram bag of your favourite chocolate and vanilla sandwich cookies (about 45 cookies in the bag)

The cookies need to be broken up as much as possible by doing one of the following:
Using a blender - blend the whole bag of cookies until they are fine crumbs as much as possible – remove any larger pieces that didn't blend and use a rolling pin to crush them.
OR
Put a few broken up cookies at a time into a sealable plastic bag and seal the bag 'almost' completely (leaving a small opening so air can escape). Use a rolling pin to crush the cookies.

Remove ½ cup of crumbs and set aside.

Put the rest of the crumbs in a deep bowl and add:
1- 250g block of softened cream cheese and blend with an electric beater until it forms a dough. No need to refrigerate the dough, but form into 1-inch balls and place in refrigerator for a few hours or overnight.

Chocolate Coating
In top of double boiler, melt 2 cups chocolate chips with ¼ bar of cooking wax or 1/3 cup cooking wax granules. Another choice would be to add 2 tablespoons of shortening instead of the cooking wax.

Use a fork or a skewer and take a ball and using a spoon – spoon the melted chocolate over the ball and place on a parchment lined cookie sheet. Continue in this fashion until they're all done. Recipe makes about 3 dozen truffles. Sprinkle each ball with the reserved crumbs.

CRISPY CRUNCH SQUARES

In a 2-quart pot, stir together:
1 cup white sugar
1 cup corn syrup
Stirring well, bring the mixture just to the boil.

Remove from heat and add 1½ cups peanut butter. Mix well and add 4 cups crispy rice cereal.

Spread out on a large piece of parchment paper OR on a buttered cookie sheet until about ¼ inch thickness.

Mix together 1 pkg. butterscotch chips and 1 pkg. chocolate chips. Put in microwave and melt using ½ power on microwave (so chocolate won't cook). Keep checking and stirring – after every minute or so. Spread this over base and leave on counter to set for a couple of hours. Don't refrigerate while it is setting – otherwise the chocolate topping may separate from the bottom.

If using parchment paper, the squares are easily cut with a pizza cutter. If using a cookie sheet, use a sharp knife.

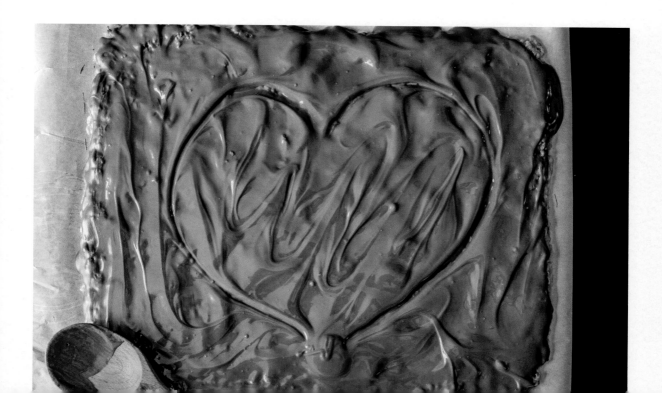

Chocolate Truffles

In a 1- or 2-quart saucepan, melt ¾ cup salted butter and then add ¾ cup cocoa (sifted) – and stir well over medium heat (with a small whisk is best). Add 1 (300 ml) can sweetened condensed milk. Stir with a whisk for about 2-3 minutes. Remove from heat and add 1 tablespoon vanilla. Stir and place in a glass bowl (uncovered) in the refrigerator until cool – then cover with plastic wrap for at least 4 hours to set.

Coating Options:
Make into one-inch balls and then roll in some crushed pecans.
OR
Coat a silicone (best option) or plastic mold, using a small artist's paint brush with chocolate melting wafers (available at bulk food stores) or use semi-sweet chocolate chips (containing cocoa butter) that have been melted with 1 tablespoon shortening. Place mold in fridge for 5 minutes. Remove from fridge and repeat the coating of chocolate. Return to the fridge for 5 minutes.

Remove from fridge and take a small amount of filling (maybe ½ teaspoon) and put into the chocolate lined mold. Don't over fill with the filling – leave some room at the top. Once all cavities are filled, add some of the melted chocolate on top of each one. When finished all, scrape off the excess. Return to the fridge for about 20 minutes or an hour.

Pop out of mold and wrap in candy foil.

So delicious!

Date Squares

Date Mixture
500-gram box pitted cooking dates (chopped)
1 cup water
Dash of salt
1 teaspoon lemon juice and a little vanilla

Put all the ingredients into a pot (except the lemon juice/vanilla). Cook over medium heat until soft (about 6 minutes). Remove from heat and add lemon juice and vanilla. Set aside.

Base and Topping
1¾ cup rolled oats (quick oats, minute oats, or regular oats)
1 1/3 cup all-purpose flour (or 1 1/3 cup whole wheat flour)
¾ cup salted butter
1 teaspoon baking soda
½ teaspoon salt
1 cup brown sugar

Mix well together.

Firmly press half mixture into a 9x9 inch pan that has been lined with parchment paper (spray a little cooking spray on sides and let the parchment paper hang over the sides). Spoon dates over base. Put the rest of the rolled oats mixture on the top and press lightly.

Bake at 350 F for 25 minutes. Cool these squares for at least 4 hours before removing from pan – use the parchment paper to lift squares out of pan and then cut into squares with a pizza cutter. Makes about 16 squares.

BROWNIES

(With optional variations)

This recipe has a couple of options including plain old brownies or a marbled cream cheese addition which I recommend highly!! You choose what you'd like. If adding the cream cheese option, make this cream cheese batter first:

Cream Cheese batter:
1–250-gram block of cream cheese softened at room temperature
1 egg
2 tablespoons sugar
1 tablespoon all-purpose flour
Using your electric beater and a small bowl – mix up the cream cheese and then add the egg and sugar and flour all at once – and continue to beat until smooth.

Brownie Batter:
Dry Ingredients
Sift the following together and set aside:
1 ½ cup all-purpose flour
1/2 cup cocoa powder
1/2 teaspoon salt

In a microwavable bowl place:
1 cup semi-sweet chocolate chips – melt in microwave

In another microwavable bowl place:
1 cup butter – melt in microwave

In a large bowl, place:
2½ cups white sugar
4 eggs
2 tsp. vanilla

Whisk until combined. Then add the melted chocolate and 1 cup melted butter and mix well.

Add the dry ingredients and mix with a whisk until combined.
Optional: Stir in ½ cup chopped walnuts.

Pour the batter into a parchment lined 9x13 inch pan and if desired sprinkle with an optional 1 cup semi-sweet chocolate chips. OR, hold on!!! If you're adding the cream cheese mixture – go to the next step.

Optional cream cheese batter: Pour the cream cheese mixture randomly over the brownie batter and using a knife, swirl it around to give it a marbleized effect. Then, as an option, sprinkle 1 cup chocolate chips over the top.
Bake in a 350 F oven for 35 minutes. Check at the 30-minute mark. If a cake tester comes out clean, remove the brownies from the oven.

Place the pan on cookie rack for 15 minutes. When time is up, use a knife along the edge and then lift out the brownies holding on to the parchment paper edges. Let cool to room temperature. They are fine as they are or some options would be the dust with icing sugar or frost with the following:

Frosting
In a small bowl, put 3 tablespoons soft butter, 2 tsp. vanilla, 3 tablespoons sifted cocoa powder, and a couple tablespoons hottest water. Mix until blended (squashing any lumps). Add 1 ¾ - 2 cups icing sugar and stir until blended. Spread over room temperature brownies.

Black & White Squares

In a large bowl place:
1/3 cup butter (softened) or margarine
1 cup white sugar
2 eggs (room temperature)
2 teaspoons vanilla
¾ cup flour
2 teaspoons baking powder
½ teaspoon salt
Mix well and put half the batter into another bowl.

To one of the bowls add:
3 tablespoons sifted cocoa powder
Mix well and put in prepared 8x8-inch pan that has been sprayed with a little cooking spray and draped with parchment paper.

To the second bowl add:
½ cup medium sweetened coconut
Mix well and spread over the chocolate layer.

Bake at 350 F for 30 minutes.

Prepare chocolate frosting:
In a small bowl, place 3 tablespoons soft butter, 2 tsp. vanilla, 3 tablespoons sifted cocoa powder, and a couple of tablespoons of hottest water. Mix until blended (squashing any lumps). Add 1¾ - 2 cups icing sugar and stir until blended. Spread over room temperature squares.

Seven Layer Squares

Prepare a 9x13-inch pan by spraying and covering with parchment paper.

Layers 1 & 2:   Mix 1½ cups graham wafer crumbs mixed with ½ cup melted butter and press firmly into pan.
Layer 3:   1½ cups medium sweetened coconut
Layer 4:   1 pkg. (300 g) butterscotch chips
Layer 5:   1 pkg. (300 g) semi-sweet chocolate chips
Layer 6:   ½ cup chopped walnuts (optional)
Layer 7:   1 can sweetened condensed milk (drizzle over top)

Bake at 350 F for 25 minutes until edges are brown and middle is set. Wait until the squares are completely cool and remove from pan by lifting out by parchment paper.

Don't trust your memory - live by the kitchen timer.

Lizzi's Peanut Butter Chocolate Chip Bars

In a bowl, place:
½ cup butter melted
1/3 cup peanut butter
1 egg
1 cup brown sugar
Mix well.
Add 1 teaspoon vanilla and mix again.
Add 1 cup flour (a little at a time) and mix well.
Add a package of chocolate chips* (300 g) or about 2 cups. *Reserve 3 tablespoons for topping.
Put into a greased 8x8 inch pan and sprinkle with reserved chocolate chips.
Bake at 350 F for 25-27 minutes.

Lizzi is the daughter of close family friends. She died June 22, 2021, of complications from a car accident. She was 11 years old. She loved to bake and watch *Tunes and Wooden Spoons*. We will miss her blonde curls and her quiet, sweet disposition. We love you Lizzi Jane.

Cape Breton Island/Eilean Ceap Breatainn

The attraction to Cape Breton Island is a love story thousands of years old. Crossing the Canso Causeway onto the island brings both a sense of excitement and belonging, be it your first trip or one of many. The natural beauty of the hills and valleys, the proximity to the Atlantic Ocean and Bras d'Or Lake, the abundance of wildlife, and of course, the people, all make Cape Breton the "home of our hearts."

Cape Breton Island is 175 kilometres long and 140 kilometres wide, with a population of roughly 134, 000. The original inhabitants of the island are the Mi'kmaq, who call the land. *Unama'ki - The Land of the Fog.* Over the last three hundred years or so, settlers began to arrive on the Island including the French Acadian, English, Loyalists, Irish, Dutch, Polish, Barbadian, African, and Gaels from the Highlands of Scotland. The bounty of the land and sea sustained and employed these people. Now generations later, Cape Breton is an island rich in its diversity of people, culture, and of course, food!

Desserts & Cakes

Decadent Chocolate Cake

In a bowl place the following:
2 cups all-purpose flour 2 cups white sugar
1 cup cocoa
2 teaspoons baking soda
1 teaspoon baking powder
1 teaspoon salt
Mix together and set aside.

In a larger bowl place the following:
3 eggs
1 cup buttermilk *
1 cup warm water
1/3 cup oil
1½ teaspoons vanilla
Beat all together with electric beater.
Slowly add dry ingredients and have mixer on low - once all added, mix on high for 2 minutes.

Prepare two 9-inch round pans by buttering sides and lining the bottoms of the pans with parchment paper. Divide the batter equally among the pans.

Bake at 350 F for 30-35 minutes. Let cool in pans on cooling rack for 15 minutes, then remove from the pans and cool for one hour on cooling rack.

Alternatives:
This recipe can also be used to make 24 cupcakes. Just reduce baking time to 20 minutes. I've also halved this recipe and made 12 cupcakes. If halving the recipe – you will split the 3 eggs. To do this, take 1 egg and place it in a little bowl and beat it just with a fork – then add just half of this beaten egg and 1 other whole egg to your batter (1½ eggs!!).
*To make buttermilk, put 1 tablespoon lemon juice in 1 cup milk and let stand 5 minutes.

Boiled Frosting
Put about 2 inches of water in the bottom of a double boiler and bring to a boil.

While this is coming to a boil, in a small bowl beat 3 egg whites with ½ teaspoon cream of tartar until just foamy and not stiff.

With an electric beater, slowly add 1½ cups brown sugar and mix until just blended. Slowly mix in ¼ cup of cold water until JUST combined. Pour all of this into the top pot of the double boiler.

Put the pot on top of the boiling water and turn the heat down to the lowest setting on the stove.

Turn beater on high and set the timer for 7 minutes. When 3 minutes are left on the timer, turn off stove completely and keep on beating. With one minute left add 1 teaspoon vanilla and beat for remainder of time.

Remove immediately from the double boiler and spread the icing over cake.

Krista's Carrot Cake

Bowl 1 - Dry Ingredients
Mix together and set aside:
3 cups flour
1 tablespoon baking soda
1½ tsp. salt
2 tsp. cinnamon

Bowl 2 – Carrots and Extras
Mix together and set aside:
3 cups shredded carrots (about 3 med/lg. carrots)
Optional extras: ½ cup raisins and/or pecans/walnuts

Bowl 3 – Main Batter
1¼ cup vegetable or canola oil
2/3 cup unsweetened apple sauce
1¼ cup white sugar
1¾ cup brown sugar
1 tablespoon vanilla
6 eggs

Using a beater, mix the oil and apple sauce and add the white sugar and mix well; add the brown sugar and mix well; add the vanilla. Now the eggs – one by one – mixing well after each egg. Change to a spatula and add the contents of Bowl 2. Add Bowl 1 (dry ingredients) and slowly stir in just until there is no more streaks of flour in the bowl. Pour evenly into 3 nine-inch round cake pans that have been prepared with parchment paper.

Bake at 350 F for 30 minutes (or less) and check with cake tester. Remove from oven and cool on cake racks for 15 minutes and then remove from cake pans and until room temperature (about an hour). When preparing to layer – slice the mound on the cake to make it flat so that you can layer each one on top of one another.

Cream Cheese Frosting
½ cup soft room temperature butter (take out of the fridge the night before and let stand)
2 x 250-gram blocks of cream cheese (take out of fridge the night before and let stand)
1 tablespoon vanilla
¼ tsp. salt
4 cups icing sugar
You may need 1 tbsp or so of milk if mixture feels like you need more liquid

Combine the cream cheese, vanilla, and salt using an electric beater beat well. Add the icing sugar 1 cup at a time until all incorporated. Add a little milk if required to reach desired consistency. Ice each layer of the cake and then do the sides and then the top. Have some crushed pecans ready (or walnuts) and sprinkle some on the top for garnish. Absolutely delicious.

Delicious White Cake

Makes a 3 Tier Cake OR 24 Cupcakes

Bowl # 1
1 cup soft salted butter
½ cup shortening.
Cream until fluffy
Add:
3 cups white sugar (1 cup at a time)
Add 5 whole eggs (1 at a time)
Beat well between additions.

Bowl # 2 (Dry Ingredients)
3 cups flour
2 tsp. baking powder
Mix and set aside.

Bowl # 3 (Wet Ingredients)
1 cup buttermilk*
2 tsp. vanilla

Mix some dry ingredients and then wet ingredients beginning and ending with dry ingredients. Pour into 3 prepared 9-inch cake pans (sprayed and lined with parchment), or 2 buttered or sprayed muffin tins.

Bake at 350 F for 30 minutes for cake or 20- 25 minutes for cupcakes. (Test early to be sure.)

*In place of buttermilk – put 1 tablespoon of either white vinegar or lemon juice in 1 cup milk, stir and let it sit for 5 minutes.

Butter Cream Frosting
1 cup salted butter
3½ cups icing sugar
5 tablespoon heavy cream or milk
1 tablespoon vanilla
Place all ingredients in a deep bowl and mix with electric beater.

Parchment Paper is the best!!

War Cake/Boiled Raisin Cake

In a 2-quart saucepan, place the following:
2 cups brown sugar
2 cups black tea
4 tablespoons shortening
1 teaspoon cloves
2 teaspoons cinnamon
1 teaspoon vanilla
½ teaspoon salt
1 package (or 2 cups) sticky raisins*

Bring to a boil and simmer for 5 minutes. Remove pot from heat and place in a sink of cold water for about 15 minutes to rush the cooling – or set aside until just warm or at room temperature.

In a bowl put 2½ cups flour and 2 teaspoons baking soda. Mix well and add to raisin mixture. Pour into a greased or parchment lined tube pan (or Bundt pan, or loaf pans).

Bake at 250 F for about 15 minutes, and then increase the heat to 300 F and bake for a further 55 minutes.

Remove from oven and place on cooling rack. Leave in pan for about 15 minutes and then remove the cake from the pan until cooled completely.

Wrap in plastic wrap and store in an air-tight container. Lasts in fridge for a couple of weeks, and also freezes well.

Delicious!!

*Lexia Raisins are sold at bulk food stores and are the "sticky raisins" – or use any other raisins such as Thompson raisins.

Buttermilk Cake

(Mommy's Recipe)

1 cup butter
2 cups brown sugar
1½ teaspoons baking soda dissolved in 2 cups buttermilk
1-pound raisins (I used 2¾ cups Thompson raisins)

Cream butter with brown sugar and add buttermilk and baking soda along with the raisins.

Dry Ingredients:
2 tsp. cinnamon
1 tsp. cloves
1 tsp. ginger
3 cups flour
Mix well and add to raisin mixture.

Pour into prepared tube pan (butter the sides and tube – and put parchment circle in bottom).

Bake at 350 F for 60 minutes (test with cake tester – or use thermometer and remove from oven when temperature registers around 198 degrees F).

(Opposite) A page from Mommy's scrapbook.

Butter Milk Cake

1 cup butter - ⅓ butter & shortening
2 cups brown sugar.
2 .. butter milk
1 lb. the raisins cut if large.
1½ tsp soda, dissolved in buttermilk
3 cups of flour or more.
all kinds of spices.
   Mix & bake.

            "Ginger Cookies" R. Fraser.
½ C. Molasses
½ shortening salt
½ c. br. sugar
put in sauce pan & boil 1 min. Cool.
2½ C. flour sifted.
1 egg.
1 tsp soda.
2 t. ginger
t. cloves.
Mix & Cool overnight roll & bake.

For soft cookies add ¼ cup hot water
    to soda & more flour

Pie Crust

This recipe makes enough pastry for a 2-crust pie

2 cups all-purpose flour
1 teaspoon salt
Mix together and add 2/3 cup shortening. Mix well with hands and then add 4½ tablespoons of cold water. Form into a ball and divide in half. Roll out each one sprinkling flour under the dough and on the rolling pin as needed.

This recipe can be halved if making a cream pie or one-crust pie.

Use dry measuring cups for flour and sugar.

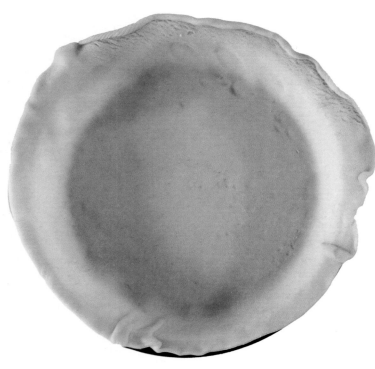

Apple Pie

5 apples sliced and put into a bowl (any kind of apple).

In a 2-cup measuring cup – place 1 cup white sugar, 3 tablespoons all-purpose flour, and 1 teaspoon cinnamon. Mix well and pour over sliced apples. Stir together and set aside while pastry is made.

Place the filling onto bottom crust and then add top crust. Trim and press edges with a fork. Prick top of crust here and there.

Bake at 375 F for 45 minutes.

Butterscotch Meringue Pie

You will need one pre-baked single pie crust.

Filling:
Have a 2-quart saucepan ready and put 3 tablespoons salted butter in it. Don't turn stove on yet.

Turn kettle on for boiling water needed later.

Measure out 1½ cups brown sugar and set aside.

Put 3 egg yolks in a medium size bowl. Put the egg whites in another bowl.

Whisk the egg yolks and set aside.

Measure 1½ cups milk and set aside.

In a larger soup bowl – put ½ cup all-purpose flour and ½ teaspoon salt – mix together.

Add a bit of the 1½ cups of milk to the eggs and whisk together. Continue to add a little flour and milk alternately until the mixture is nice and smooth and no lumps.

Turn on stove top and melt the butter over medium heat. Once melted, add the brown sugar and keep stirring for a while. The brown sugar will start turning a darker brown. Keep stirring for about 5 minutes.

Carefully add ¾ cup boiling water a little at a time. When complete, there'll be some tiny clumps of brown sugar – pour that through a sieve and return to the stove on medium heat.

Pour milk and egg mixture slowly into the brown sugar mixture and stir with a spatula until thick (about 4-5 minutes).

Let the filling cool for about 20 minutes – making sure to put a plate over the pot otherwise a skin will form on top. After about 10 minutes, take plate off and stir briefly then put plate back on for another 10 minutes. Pour into cooled pie crust and add meringue.

Meringue
Have 3 egg whites in a deep glass bowl. Have ¼ cup of sugar at the ready but don't add it yet. Beat egg whites at medium speed until frothy. Put the beater on high and start adding the ¼ cup sugar gradually until the meringue is peaky – don't over-beat. Spread on pie and make a few little peaks by placing a spoon on the meringue and lifting up.

Place pie in 400 F oven for maybe 5 minutes – watching carefully until nicely browned. Allow to cool completely. If cut too soon the filling will spill out. It needs to set until it is at room temperature.

Rhubarb Butterscotch Pie

Mommy's Recipe

3 cups chopped rhubarb
¾ cup brown sugar
3 tablespoons flour
2 eggs beaten (plus 2-3 extra egg whites for meringue)
3 tablespoons heavy cream
Dash of salt

Line pie plate with single crust pastry and fill with chopped rhubarb. Mix remaining ingredients and spread over rhubarb. Bake at 450 degrees for 10 minutes and reduce heat to 350 for 20 minutes.

Follow meringue recipe on page 66 (Butterscotch Meringue Pie)

Mama's Versatile Puddings/Pie Fillings

Basic Vanilla Pudding
1 cup white sugar, 5 tablespoons cornstarch (or 4 if you like it softer)
Mix well and add 2 cups milk. Stir over medium heat and use spatula constantly. Continue stirring until mixture thickens – and then add 1 tablespoon salted butter and 1 teaspoon vanilla.

Coconut Cream Pie Filling
Add ½ cup medium sweetened coconut to Basic Vanilla Pudding recipe before adding the milk. All the rest is the same.

Banana Cream Pie Filling
Make Basic Vanilla Pudding and put in fridge until completely cold. Mash one small banana and mix into the cold vanilla pudding. Coin another small banana and mix into the pudding. Put in baked pie shell and top with Whipped Cream or Dream Whip or Cool Whip or Meringue. Banana Pie needs to be consumed when it's made because the bananas turn dark unless you dip them in a ½ cup water and a tablespoon lemon juice

Chocolate Pudding & Pie Filling
Make Basic Vanilla Pudding but add 5 tablespoons cocoa to the white sugar and cornstarch. All the rest is the same. Serve warm with a scoop of ice cream. Delicious.

Lemon Pie from Scratch

Prepare and cook the pie crust using the single crust recipe on page 86. Set the cooked crust to cool.

In a deep narrow bowl place:
3 egg whites and set aside for the meringue.

Place egg yolks in a small bowl and mix with a fork and set aside.

Cut 2 lemons in half and juice the lemon until there's about 1/3 cup juice. Set this aside until needed.

In a medium saucepan, place the following:
9 tablespoons cornstarch
1½ cup plus 6 tablespoons white sugar
¼ teaspoon salt
Mix well.

Add 1½ cups hot water
Cook over medium/high heat until thick. Remove from heat.

Add a little of this hot batter to the 3 egg yolks and stir. Add a little more hot batter to the eggs and mix and stir, and then add all the egg mixture to the cornstarch/sugar mixture. Whisk this up and return to a low heat and stir for 6 minutes. Remove from heat.

Add 2 tablespoons salted butter and stir until butter is melted.

Add the 1/3 cup lemon juice and stir until combined.

Pour hot lemon pudding into a cooled pie crust.

Follow the meringue from the recipe on page 66 and bake as per the instructions.

Let the pie cool to room temperature before cutting as the filling needs to set. This lemon pie is SUPER tangy and lemony!

Raisin Pie

Crust:
Combine together:
2 cups flour
1 teaspoon salt
2/3 cup shortening
Blend until mixture is crumbly.

Add 5-6 tablespoons cold water sprinkled over mixture. Toss gently with fork and then form into a ball. Cut into two equal pieces and roll each one out. Roll out each one to form the bottom and top crust.

Raisin Filling:
2 cups raisins (any kind but I use Thompson raisins)
2 cups water

Combine the raisins and water in a saucepan and when it comes to a boil – continue to simmer for 5 more minutes.

In a small bowl:
½ cup packed brown sugar
2 tablespoons cornstarch
½ teaspoon cinnamon
¼ teaspoon salt

Mix well together and add to the raisin mixture after it has finished the 5-minute boil. Mix and stir until syrup is not cloudy but clear, about 1-2 minutes. Remove from heat and stir in 1 tablespoon lemon juice OR 1 tablespoon vanilla – and 1 tablespoon butter. Cool slightly. Put in pastry lined pie pan and cover with remaining pastry top. Cut off excess dough and edge as you wish (I use a fork) and prick with a fork all over the surface.

Bake at 425 F for 20 minutes or at 400 F for 30 minutes.

Serve with a scoop of vanilla ice cream. Delicious!

Ice Cream Cake

Make this 24 hours before serving. (You will need a spring form pan.)

First crush about 8-10 crunch chocolate toffee bars for use and set aside.

Mix together: 2½ cups chocolate and vanilla sandwich cookie crumbs and 2/3 cup melted salted butter.

Make a circle of parchment paper to go on the bottom of the spring form pan. Then put the cookie crumb mixture in pan. Place in freezer for 15 minutes.

Have 2 litres of two different kinds of favourite ice cream which has been softened a bit for easy spreading and put about 1 litre of the ice cream over the cookie crumb base. Sprinkle half the crunchy chocolate toffee bar pieces over this. Now put another litre or more of the ice cream on top of the candy bar pieces. Sprinkle the rest of the candy bars on top.

Put in freezer for 24 hours until ready to serve. Serve out of the freezer and top with a warm caramel sauce. (See Mama's Caramel Sauce, page 152.)

CREAM CHEESE TARTS

Tart Shells
Use 24 frozen tart shells for this recipe. Follow directions on back of box to cook the tarts: separate the tarts and let thaw on counter for 10 minutes and place on cookie sheet for about 12 minutes at 375 F.

Filling
1-250-gram block softened cream cheese
1 cup of white sugar
1 teaspoon lemon juice

Put all above in a bowl and beat with electric beater. Set aside.

Whip up 1 packet whipped topping mix with ½ cup cold milk and 1 teaspoon vanilla. With electric beater on low, add whipped topping to cream cheese mixture until just blended. Spoon the mixture into cooled tarts – there's enough to fill 24 tarts exactly. Cut up your favourite fruits for garnish (kiwi, mandarin oranges, blueberries, raspberries, strawberries) or drizzle with homemade chocolate or caramel sauce.

German Apple Cake

Whisk together:
3 large eggs
1 cup oil
2 cups white sugar
1 teaspoon vanilla

In a separate bowl, mix:
2 cups all-purpose flour
2 teaspoons cinnamon
1 teaspoon soda
Mix well and add to egg mixture.

Add 1 cup raisins
3 large peeled and wedged Granny Smith apples
(or 4 small)
Pour into a greased/floured 9-inch spring-form pan
or line with parchment paper.

Bake at 350 F for 55 - 60 minutes.

While the cake is baking, mix the cream cheese
topping.

Cream Cheese Topping
1-250-gram block of cream cheese, softened
2 tablespoons soft salted butter
2 teaspoons vanilla
Dash of salt
2 cups icing sugar
Put all together in a bowl and blend with an electric beater.

When cake is done, remove from the oven and
pour the cream cheese topping on the hot cake
and return to the 350 F oven for about 18 minutes
(or fewer) to caramelize the topping.

Remove from oven and put on cooling rack until
cake is completely cool. Slide sharp knife around all
the edges and open the spring lock and slide cake
onto cooling rack. Slide knife under cake and slide
cake onto rack (removing the parchment paper).
Slice in small wedges with a dollop of whipped
cream (whipped with a teaspoon of vanilla).

Bread Pudding
(Recipe is for 8 x 8 pan. Double recipe for 9 x 13 pan)

Sweets

Desserts

Bread Pudding

6 slices day-old bread
2 tablespoons melted salted butter
½ cup raisins
4 beaten eggs
2 cups milk
¾ cup white sugar
1 teaspoon cinnamon
1 teaspoon vanilla

Pull apart the bread in bite sized pieces and put in an 8x8-inch pan and mix in the raisins. Drizzle with the melted butter. Combine the remaining ingredients and pour over the bread and lightly push down with a fork until the bread is covered and soaking up the egg mixture.

Bake at 350 F for 45 minutes. The pudding will be raised up to nearly the top of the pan, but let it settle down for about 25 minutes before serving. Serve with a dollop of whipped cream that a teaspoon of vanilla has been added to. Also great with a wee splash of Mama's Caramel Sauce (page 152).

Rhubarb Pudding Dessert

Grease a 9x9 inch square pan with salted butter
or spray.
Cut rhubarb to make 3 cups.

In a bowl place:
2/3 cup melted salted butter
1/3 cup milk
½ teaspoon vanilla
Mix well.

In another bowl place:
1 cup all-purpose flour
2/3 cup white sugar
1 teaspoon baking powder
¼ teaspoon salt
Mix and add to butter mixture. Mix well and spread
over rhubarb.

Mix together 1 cup icing sugar and 1 tablespoon
cornstarch. Mix and spread over batter in pan. Pour
1 cup of cold water over batter.

Bake at 350 F for 1 hour. Serve warm with a scoop
of vanilla ice cream.

Hot Fudge Sundae Cake

Dry Ingredients:
1 cup all-purpose flour
¾ cup white sugar
2 tablespoons cocoa
2 teaspoons baking powder
¼ teaspoon salt
Mix well and set aside.

Wet Ingredients:
½ cup milk
2 tablespoons oil (canola or vegetable)
1 teaspoon vanilla
Mix well and add to dry ingredients and spread in lightly greased 9x9 inch pan. Set aside.

Topping:
In a small bowl mix up 1 cup brown sugar and ¼ cup cocoa. Sprinkle this mixture over the batter in the pan. Pour 1¾ cups of hottest (almost boiling) water over the brown sugar and cocoa mixture. DO NOT STIR!! The water mixture on top sinks into the batter and creates a sauce underneath the brownie batter once it's baked.

Carefully transfer the pan to 350 F oven for 40 minutes.

Serve hot from oven with a scoop of vanilla ice cream. Delicious!!

If a recipe calls for room temperature butter, your eggs should be room temperature too.

Caramel Cheesecake

Prepare a 9-inch spring-form pan with parchment paper lining the bottom only. Then wrap foil wrap around the bottom of the pan and up the sides to protect it from the water bath when it is in the oven. Crease up any edges of the foil so no water can seep in.

1 cup graham wafer crumbs
1 tablespoon melted salted butter
Press into the spring-form pan and set aside.

In a deep bowl beat:
3 -250-gram (8 ounce) blocks cream cheese, at room temperature
Gradually add mixing but not over-mixing:
1 cup white sugar
1 cup sour cream (250-gram tub)
1 teaspoon vanilla
Then add 3 eggs, one at a time until just combined. Pour this batter into the prepared crust.

Place spring form pan into a larger dish that has sides on it. Prepare the water bath by filling the exterior pan with boiling water until it comes about 1" up the sides of the spring-form pan. Baking the cheesecake in a water bath prevents it from splitting.

Place cheesecake in 325 F oven. Bake for 10 minutes. Then, reduce heat to 300 F and bake for another hour plus 15 minutes. Don't remove cake from the oven – but turn the heat off and let the cheesecake stay in the oven for about 30 minutes. Open the oven door a bit and let it sit for another 10 minutes.

Carefully remove the spring form pan from the water bath and place cheesecake on a cooling rack. Slide a knife all around the edges of the cheesecake. Let it cool at room temperature for about 1 hour and before placing in the fridge. Run the knife around the edge just to make sure it's not sticking and then place in the fridge for at least 4 hours before serving. Now is a good time to make Mama's Caramel Sauce, page 152, which needs to be served at room temperature or cold. OR serve the cheesecake with a favourite fruit topping.

Sticky Toffee Pudding

Bowl # 1
2 cups + 2 tablespoons all-purpose flour
2 teaspoons baking soda
Mix soda into the flour and set aside.

Bowl # 2 (larger bowl)
1½ cups of pitted dates (chopped)
Sprinkle 2 teaspoons baking soda over dates
Pour 2½ cups boiling water over the top
Stir date mixture and set aside.

Bowl # 3 (larger bowl)
½ cup softened salted butter
1½ cups white sugar
2 eggs
2 teaspoons vanilla
Mix with an electric mixer

Once the ingredients in Bowl # 3 are well beaten, slowly begin to add the flour mixture. When all the flour mixture is added and mixed, fold all this mixture into Bowl # 2 (the date mixture). This mixture will be quite loose but that's okay. Keep mixing and using the back of the spatula to squash down the pieces of the mixture.

Pour the batter into a greased (or parchment lined) 9x13 inch pan.

Bake at 350 F for 35-40 minutes. Remove from oven and let cool.

Serve with Mama's Caramel Sauce (see page 152) and garnish with a dollop of whipped cream or a scoop of vanilla ice cream.

Pumpkin Roll Dessert

In a large bowl:
3 eggs yolks (put the whites into a separate deep bowl)
½ cup white sugar
2/3 cup pumpkin puree (canned or fresh)
Beat egg yolks well. Gradually add sugar and the pumpkin.
Mix well and set aside.

In deep bowl:
3 eggs whites
Beat until foamy, and gradually add ½ cup sugar until soft peaks form.
Fold the egg whites into the pumpkin mixture.

In a separate bowl:
¾ cup all-purpose flour
1 teaspoon baking soda
½ teaspoon cinnamon
¼ teaspoon salt
Mix well and fold into pumpkin/egg mixture.

Cover a 16x10 inch cookie sheet with parchment paper. Pour batter into pan.

Place in 375 F oven for 15-17 minutes or until cake springs back when touched in the middle. (It is a good idea to turn the pan around halfway through baking.) Watch the cake carefully to make sure it does not overcook.

Filling:
1-250-gram brick cream cheese, softened
2 tablespoons soft salted butter
1 teaspoon vanilla
1½ cups icing sugar (powdered sugar)

Put all ingredients in a bowl and beat with an electric mixer until well combined. Set aside.

When cake is done, **cool 5 minutes only** on cooling rack. Lay a tea towel on the counter and using a sieve, sprinkle with some icing sugar. After the cake has cooled for 5 minutes – lay the cake upside down on top of tea towel and remove the parchment paper. Roll up cake (from the shorter side) **along with the dish towel** and put in refrigerator until completely chilled – this will take about 45 minutes.

Unroll cake and spread cream cheese filling over the cake. Roll up like a jelly roll (without the dishtowel this time). Cover securely with plastic wrap and chill for at least 2 hours.

Remove from plastic wrap and sprinkle with a bit more icing sugar. Slice and serve with a garnish of whipped cream. This can be frozen but remove from freezer at least 15 minutes before serving.

Fruit Pizza

Glaze:
Make glaze first and put in refrigerator to cool.
To ½ cup sugar add 2 ½ teaspoons cornstarch and mix.
Add ½ cup water and ½ cup orange juice.
Mix well and put in saucepan. Heat to boiling stirring constantly. Once the mixture comes to a boil, let it boil for 1 minute. Remove from heat and refrigerate.

Crust:
Butter a cookie sheet or pizza pan or cover with parchment paper. Mix the following well:
½ cup soft butter
1½ cups brown sugar
1 cup medium sweetened coconut
1½ cups rolled oats
1 cup all-purpose flour
1 teaspoon baking powder
1 teaspoon baking soda

Beat 1 egg with 1 tsp. vanilla. Add to rolled oats mixture and stir until it forms a dough.
Spread out on prepared cookie sheet.

Bake at 350 F for 8 to 10 minutes. It should be brown along the edges but puffed up and wiggly in the middle – take it out then and it will settle. If left in even 2 minutes longer it will settle down and will be hard as a rock. Don't do that. Cool for 25 minutes until slightly warm.

Cream Cheese Filling:
2 – 250-gram blocks cream cheese, softened
2/3 cups white sugar
1 teaspoon vanilla
Beat with electric beater and spread over cooled crust.

Fruit Topping
Slice strawberries, bananas, kiwi, blueberries, raspberries – any fruit of choice. If using bananas, put 1/3 cup lemon or orange juice in ¾ cup cold water and place bananas in for a couple of minutes to avoid browning. Arrange the fruit to your liking all over the cream cheese topping.

Once fruit is arranged, take the chilled glaze and drizzle over all. Refrigerate for at least 1 hour. This dessert is best the first day and may still be okay the second day but after that the crust begins to get soggy. Also, if you want it to last at least two to three days, don't bother with bananas.

MANDARIN ORANGE DESSERT

In a mixing bowl put the following dry ingredients and mix together:
1 cup white sugar
1 cup all-purpose flour
1 teaspoon baking soda
¼ teaspoon salt

In a smaller bowl put the following:
1 egg - beat it well with a whisk.
Add the juice from the can of mandarin oranges (284 ml /10 ounce can)
Mix well and add to the dry ingredients and mix well.

Add the mandarin oranges and stir.

Pour into a greased 9x9 inch pan (cooking spray is easy).

Bake at 350 F and bake for about 35-37 minutes.

Topping:
Before the cake is done, mix in a small bowl:
¾ cup brown sugar
2 tablespoons soft salted butter
2 tablespoons of milk

Stir this well and as soon as the cake is done, remove from the oven and lightly spread the whole mixture over the top.

Return to the 350 F oven for about 10 minutes or until the topping is bubbling all over. Remove from oven and let it come to room temperature. Serve with a dollop of whipped cream or a small scoop of vanilla ice cream. Delicious.

Read the recipe through to the end before you start.

Five Layer Lemon Squares/Dessert

Layer One:
2 cup graham wafer crumbs
½ cup salted butter (melted)
Mix well and press into place in a greased 9x9 inch pan.

Layer Two:
Half brick softened cream cheese (125 g)
½ cup white sugar
4 tablespoons frozen whipped topping
Mix well and spread over Layer One.

Layer Three:
Cook 1 package lemon pie filling and cool to room temperature.
Pour half the cooled batter over Layer Two.

Layer Four:
1½ cups frozen whipped topping mixed folded with ½ package room temperature lemon pie filling.
Spread over Layer Three.

Layer Five:
Spread whipped topping over Layer Four.
Sprinkle some graham wafer crumbs over top and refrigerate for at least 2 hours before serving.

Apple Crisp

In a buttered 9x9 inch pan, slice 5-6 medium sized apples

Mix together until crumbly:
1½ cups all-purpose flour
1½ cups rolled oats
1½ cup brown sugar
2 teaspoons cinnamon
¾ cup salted butter

Take half the mixture and add to the apples and mix well.

Take the other half and put over the top of the apple mixture. Pat down.

Bake at 350 F for about 40 minutes. Serve warm with a scoop of vanilla ice cream.

So easy and so good.

Gingerbread Cake

First things first:
Put kettle on to boil.
Spray a 9x9 inch pan with cooking spray and then lay parchment paper across the pan – letting it hang over the sides. This will help later when taking the cake out of the pan.

Batter:
½ cup shortening
2 tablespoons white sugar
1 room temperature egg
Mix this together.

In a separate bowl place:
1 cup molasses
1 cup boiling water
Stir until molasses is dissolved and then add to shortening mixture and mix well.

In another bowl place:
2½ cups all-purpose flour
½ teaspoon salt
1 teaspoon baking soda
1 teaspoon ground ginger
1 teaspoon cinnamon

Mix well and add slowly to batter, beating slowly to combine. Pour batter into prepared pan.

Bake at 325 F for 40-45 minutes or until the top is firm.

Remove to cooling rack and if using parchment paper, lift out of pan. If not, leave in the pan to cool. May be served warm with Mama's Caramel Sauce (see page 152). To make it a rum sauce, add ¼ cup rum.

Mini Cheesecakes with Raspberry Sauce

Crust:
¾ cup graham wafer crumbs
2½ tablespoons melted butter
1 tablespoon white sugar
Mix well and add 1½ tablespoons to a lined muffin pan. Makes 12.

Cheesecake:
1-250-gram block of cream cheese, softened
1/3 cup white sugar
1 teaspoon vanilla
Zest of ½ lemon (optional)
Beat these ingredients until well mixed.
Add 1 egg and beat until smooth.
Then add 1/3 cup whipping cream (unwhipped)
Pour onto graham cracker bases in muffin tin.

Bake at 300 F for 18 minutes.

Raspberry Sauce:
1½ cups fresh raspberries (or frozen)
¼ cup white sugar
3 tablespoons water
Place in small saucepan over low heat and simmer gently for about 10 minutes. Stir ever so gently. When 10 minutes is up, add 1½ teaspoons cornstarch which has been dissolved in about a teaspoon of cold water and pour over raspberries. Continue to cook on low heat and stir for 1 minute. Cool to room temperature.

Serve each mini cheesecake with some raspberry sauce and a dollop of whipped cream OR a nice option is a few spoons of Mama's Caramel Sauce on page 152.

Layered Chocolate Delight

Layer One (Shortbread Base)
¾ cup butter or margarine
1½ cup flour
½ cup chopped pecans (or walnuts)
Mix together and put in a sprayed (or buttered) 9 x 13-inch pan.

Bake at 350 F for 15-18 minutes and set aside to cool.

Layer Two
1 250 - gram block cream cheese, softened
1 cup icing sugar
½ container (1 litre) of frozen whipped topping OR 1 cup of whipping cream, whipped
Beat with an electric beater and then spread this on top of the cooled shortbread base.

Layer Three
1 package INSTANT vanilla pudding (serves 4)
1 package INSTANT chocolate pudding (serves 4)
2 ½ cups milk
Beat with electric beater for 2-3 minutes until it thickens. Spread over cream cheese layer.

Layer Four
Spread the other ½ container of frozen whipped topping or 1 cup of whipping cream, whipped, over the top.

Layer Five
Garnish with grated semi-sweet chocolate or your favourite chocolate bar.
Cover with plastic wrap and refrigerate for one hour before cutting. So good.

Port Hood/Seastago

Port Hood is the village where I've lived for the past fifty years. It's where Cecil and I made our home and where we raised our seven beautiful children. It's where I continued to learn lots of recipes from my mother-in-law, Marie. It is a beautiful and welcoming community, and it is my home.

Historically, Port Hood has been a centre for fishing, boat building, quarrying stone for the Fortress of Louisbourg, family and coal mining. It became established as a political centre on the west side of the island and is now home to the headquarters for the Municipality of Inverness County. Today,

an elementary school, hockey rink, museum, local churches and a variety of businesses contribute to this vibrant, rural village.

The community has some of the most beautiful coastlines to be seen on the western side of the island, with five beaches to its credit. Locals and tourists alike can be seen flocking to the nearby seaside during the summer months. The Chestico Days festival held on the first weekend of August every year, is a highlight of everyone's year - a lively gathering of family, friends and hospitality.

SALADS, SOUPS & QUICK MEALS

Quinoa Salad

Cook 1 cup plain quinoa in 2 cups water. Let it come to a boil and then simmer for about 20 minutes until absorbed. Put in refrigerator until cool.

Add:
1-2 handfuls cut up spinach
Some crumbled feta cheese
½ cup diced peppers (red/orange/yellow)
½ red onion diced
½ English cucumber diced
1 cup chopped tomatoes
Mix well and then add dressing.

Dressing
¼ cup olive oil
¼ cup balsamic vinegar OR red wine vinegar
1 teaspoon lemon juice
1 teaspoon honey
½ teaspoon dried oregano
½ teaspoon salt
½ teaspoon pepper
Mix well and pour over quinoa. Place in fridge until cold.

Broccoli and Cauliflower Salad

1 fresh broccoli – cut into bite size pieces
1 fresh cauliflower – cut into bite size pieces
1 sliced onion (leave in rings)
1 green pepper sliced
1 red pepper sliced
1 cup grated cheddar cheese
½ cup real bacon pieces
Mix above in large salad bowl.

Dressing
1 cup real mayonnaise
¼ cup white sugar
4 tablespoons white vinegar.
Mix well and mix into salad. Cover, refrigerate,
serve cold.

Spinach Salad with Maple Dressing

(Two options)

Dressing
1 cup real mayonnaise
¼ cup maple syrup
½ teaspoon dry mustard
2 tablespoons white vinegar
Dash of pepper
Mix and put in Mason jar and shake before using.

Salad 1
Spinach
Boiled eggs
Red Onion
Mandarin Oranges
Bacon
Mix in whatever quantity and drizzle with dressing.

Salad 2
Spinach
Red Onion
Sliced Strawberries
Yellow Pepper
Walnuts
Mix in whatever quantity and drizzle with dressing.

Ratatouille

Prepare vegetables as follows:
1 eggplant (diced) (optional)
1 medium onion cut in ½ inch chunks
1 red pepper cut in ½ inch wide strips
2 medium zucchini cut into ½ inch chunks

Put chopped veggies in large frying pan and drizzle over them 2 tablespoons of your favourite sundried tomato and oregano dressing. Sauté over medium heat and stir for 5 minutes or so.

Add 1 can diced tomatoes and stir occasionally for about another 15 minutes.

Pour vegetable mixture into a 9x13 inch pan and sprinkle with ¼ cup Parmesan cheese and ¼ cup shredded mozzarella cheese.

Bake at 350 F for about 15 minutes (or until cheese is melted).

Irish Potato Soup

2 tablespoons butter
1 medium onion (grated)
2 pounds russet potatoes, peeled and diced (about 4 large potatoes)
3 cups chicken stock
1 teaspoon kosher salt
½ teaspoon garlic powder
¼ teaspoon ground black pepper
2 cups whole milk
Some parsley for garnish (optional)

Melt butter in a Dutch oven over medium heat. Sauté the grated onion for 5 minutes or until tender. Add the potatoes, garlic powder, kosher salt and pepper and chicken stock. Bring to a boil and reduce the heat to low. Simmer for 20-25 minutes or until the potatoes are soft. Use an immersion blender and blend until the potato mixture is smooth and creamy.

When mixture is smooth, add the milk. Taste and add more salt and pepper if needed. Sprinkle a little parsley over the top. Serve immediately. You can add chopped, cooked bacon and/or corn kernels as a garnish.

Parsnip and Carrot Pureed Soup

Melt ¼ cup butter in a large fry pan

Add:
2 large onions diced, and sauté over medium/high heat until golden (about 15 minutes).

Add:
4 large carrots cubed (about 1-inch cubes)
4 large parsnips (about 1-inch cubes)

Sauté with onions for about 10 minutes and set aside.

In Dutch oven size pot, put 1 large container of chicken broth (about 900 ml) and add 3 large raw potatoes cut into 1-inch cubes, add some parsley and thyme. Add the other vegetables and bring to a boil and then simmer for 30 minutes. Remove from heat.

Puree the soup using an immersion blender (or blender). Add a 500 ml container of blend cream (or about 1½ cups any cream). Season with salt and pepper. Can be prepared a day ahead. Cover and refrigerate and when ready to serve – bring slowly to heat. Serve with a sprig of parsley and a small dollop of sour cream. So delicious.

Roasted Red Pepper Tomato Soup

3 ripe tomatoes
3 cloves garlic
½ large onion
1 red pepper
1 tablespoon olive oil
1–28 ounce can stewed tomatoes
3-4 tablespoons tomato paste
Sea salt and black pepper
1 cup low sodium vegetable broth
½ cup milk

Preheat oven to 375 F.
Cut tomatoes and onions into wedges and remove some of the seeds. Remove seeds from red pepper and cut into even slices. Place all the veggies including the garlic on baking sheet and drizzle with olive oil, a generous pinch of sea salt and black pepper and toss. Roast for about 40-45 minutes or until veggies are tender, lightly browned, and close to half their original size. Remove from oven and set aside.

In a large pot over medium heat, add canned tomatoes, veggie broth, tomato paste, the roasted veggies, and more salt and pepper. Bring to a low boil. Reduce heat and simmer 10 minutes. Puree with immersion blender. Add ½ cup milk or cream and simmer 5-10 minutes on low heat.

Easy Corn Chowder

Boil 5 potatoes (with skins on) until cooked through. Peel and dice potatoes and set aside.

In a frying pan, place
5 slices cooked ham cut up into small squares
½ onion grated
Fry together until lightly browned.

In a Dutch oven place:
The boiled, peeled, and diced potatoes
2 cans creamed corn (398 ml cans)
2 cans kernel corn (341 ml cans)
Diced ham and onions.

Add 2½ cups whole milk and stir. Add 1 tsp. salt and some pepper. Heat to scalding and serve.

Hamburger Soup

In a Dutch oven, cook together until done:
1½ pounds ground beef
1 medium onion grated well
Drain well.

To the cooked beef and onion mixture, add:
1–28 ounce can diced tomatoes
2 cups water
1 box beef broth (946 ml)
1 can tomato soup
4 carrots, coined
3 stalks celery, chopped
2 medium potatoes, diced
Shake of dried parsley
½ tsp. thyme
Pepper to taste
8 tablespoons barley

Simmer covered for at least 2 hours. Serves 10.

Delicious.

Greek yogurt is a healthy substitute for mayo, sour cream, and heavy cream.

CREAMY SCALLOPED POTATOES

Wash, peel, and slice 10 medium sized potatoes and place into a well-buttered 9x13 inch pan until, the potatoes are about ½ inch from the top.

In a saucepan, melt 3 tablespoons butter
Whisk in 3 tablespoons flour.
Add 1 tsp. salt and some ground pepper.
Add 2½ cups milk and 1 small onion grated fine.
Continue whisking until mixture comes to a boil and is thickening a bit and then pour over the potatoes. Cover with foil wrap.

Bake at 350 F for 1½ hours (or until tender).
Remove foil for the last 15-20 minutes of bake time.

Easy Spaghetti Sauce

In a Dutch oven, brown 1½ pounds ground beef with 1 tsp. each of onion powder and garlic powder. Add salt and pepper to taste.

When the meat is browned, add:
2 bottles favourite spaghetti sauce
1 large can tomato sauce
1 can diced tomatoes
Add Italian seasoning, oregano, and basil. Simmer for 15 minutes.

Easy Oven Baked Rice Casserole

2 cups long grain brown rice
¼ cup soya sauce
½ cup green pepper diced
4 cups water
1 package onion soup mix
¼ cup oil
½ cup celery
1 can drained mushroom slices.

Spray 9x13 inch pan with cooking spray. Place each ingredient in the pan and then stir gently. Cover tightly with foil.

Bake at 350 F for 1 hour. Remove foil and stir.

Invest in a baking mat.

Hash Brown Casserole

1– 2-pound bag frozen hash browns (the larger chunks)
½ onion well-grated
1 can cream of chicken soup
2 cups sour cream
1 cup grated cheddar cheese
Salt and pepper
1 cup corn flakes
½ cup melted butter

Mix soup, onion, sour cream, cheddar cheese and add to hash browns. Stir well and sprinkle with salt and pepper. Pour into a buttered 9 x 13-inch pan. Sprinkle 1 cup corn flakes over top and drizzle with ½ cup melted butter. Cover tightly with foil wrap.

Bake at 350 F for 1 hour.

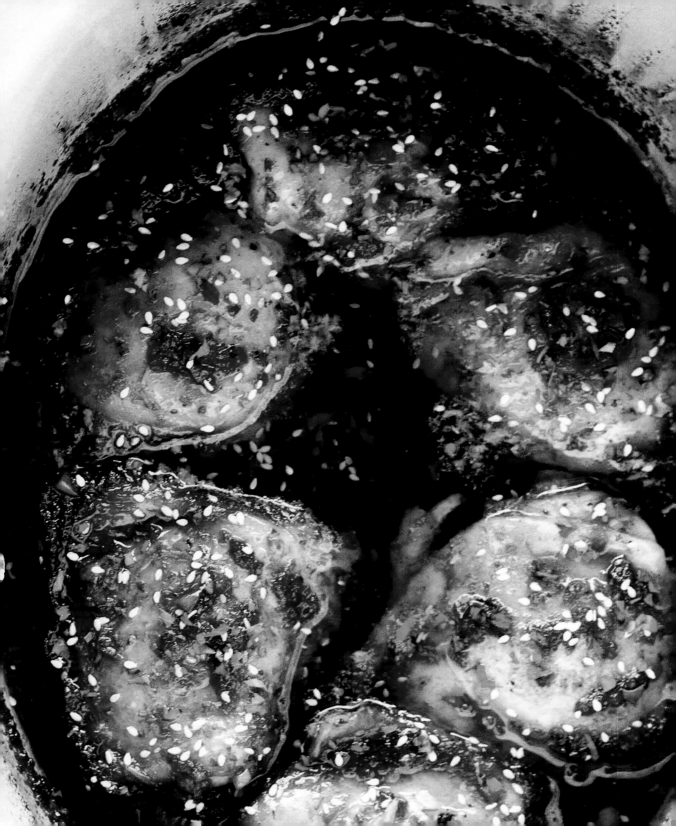

Marjorie's Slow Cooker Honey Garlic Chicken

6 boneless skinless chicken thighs (or chicken of choice)
4 minced garlic cloves
1/3 cup honey
½ cup ketchup
½ cup soy sauce
½ teaspoon oregano
2 tablespoons parsley

Place chicken in bottom of slow cooker and set aside. Mix all the rest in a bowl. Pour over chicken. Cook for 4-5 hours on low or 3-4 hours on high.

Cornflake Chicken and Alfredo Sauce

5 large boneless chicken breasts

Prepare the chicken breasts by using the bottom of a glass and flattening the chicken so that each breast is approximately the same height. Cut each breast in half to make 10 pieces. Set aside.

Prepare a stoneware or cookie sheet with parchment paper and set aside.

Bowl 1:
8 heaping tablespoons real mayonnaise with 1 cup parmesan cheese and mix together. Set aside.

Bowl 2:
Put 2 cups or so of cornflakes into a sealable bag and crush with rolling pin. Add 1 tablespoon Italian seasoning and mix well. Place in Bowl 2.

Method:
Take each chicken breast and with a spoon, coat each piece of chicken with the mayo mixture, and then roll in the cornflake crumbs and place on prepared pan.

Melt a little butter and drizzle over each chicken breast.

Place in 375 F oven for about 40-45 minutes. If you choose, shred some mozzarella cheese over the chicken 5 minutes before it's done.

Check for doneness – thermometer should reach 165 degrees F.

10-Minute Alfredo Sauce

Melt 3 heaping tablespoons butter and 3 cloves minced garlic. Add a 500-gram box of Blend cream. Add a ½ tub or ½ of a 250-gram package of softened cream cheese and whisk well until no lumps. Add 1 cup parmesan cheese and stir until heated through. Cover and remove from heat until fettucine noodles are cooked and chicken is ready.

To Serve:
Cook fettucine noodles until done. In another pot, heat up a large can of your favourite tomato sauce and add some Italian seasoning, oregano, and basil, and stir until heated. Place chicken on plate and cover with tomato sauce. Pour Alfredo sauce over the noodles. Good side dishes to accompany include Ratatouille (see recipe on page 122) and Herb Bread (recipe on page 20).

CREAMY BAKED CHICKEN

8 boneless chicken breasts
8 Swiss cheese slices
2 cans cream of chicken soup
¼ cup wine or water
1 box stove top stuffing
1/3 cup melted butter

Using a glass, flatten the chicken until the pieces are fairly even in height. Place chicken in a 9x13 inch pan. Cover each breast with a slice of Swiss cheese. Mix the soup and water in a bowl and then spread over the cheese and chicken. Sprinkle the uncooked stove top stuffing over all the chicken and then sprinkle with the melted butter.

Bake at 350 F for 55-60 minutes, uncovered. Use a thermometer to check that the chicken has reached 165 F.

Chicken Cordon Bleu

5 boneless chicken breasts

In a bowl, mix 1 tablespoon garlic powder, 1 tablespoon onion powder, ½ teaspoon salt, ½ teaspoon pepper.

Sprinkle the mixed spices over the chicken and massage until covered on all sides. Take each chicken breast (one at a time) and place between plastic wrap on top of a cutting board and using a mallet or rolling pin, roll out and pound until each breast is about ½ inch thick. Take each breast and put 1 slice of Swiss cheese and 1 or 2 slices black forest ham and then roll up and wrap tightly with plastic wrap and place on a tray. Continue with each breast until all 5 breasts are done and wrapped and place in the refrigerator for 30 minutes.

Meanwhile, preheat a tall-sided frying pan with about 1½ inches of canola oil heated to about 325 F degrees. After the chicken rolls have been refrigerated for the 30 minutes, have 3 bowls ready:
1st bowl: 1 cup flour
2nd bowl: 3 eggs well-beaten
3rd bowl: 2 cups breadcrumbs

Have a tray ready to place your chicken on. Take each chicken roll and roll in the flour, then the beaten eggs, and then the breadcrumbs and place on a tray. Place all the chicken, into the frying pan and cook for 5 minutes, then flip once, and cook another 5 minutes. Using a thermometer, check to make sure the internal temperature of the chicken has reached 165 degrees F.

When the chicken is cooked, remove from oil and place on a wire rack (over a cookie sheet to catch drips). If the chicken **has not** reached 165 F after frying, place on a parchment lined cookie sheet and place in a 325 oven until internal temperature is reached.

Sauce: (optional)
In a 2-quart saucepan, put 3 tablespoons butter and 3 cloves minced garlic and sauté til garlic is soft. Add 3 tablespoons flour and whisk until absorbed. Add 2 cups milk and whisk until there are no lumps and the sauce begins to thicken. Add 1 cup shredded parmesan cheese and mix well. Optional: add ¼ cup Dijon mustard. Season with salt and pepper. Remove from heat. Take each chicken breast and slice each roll about 1-inch pieces (being careful not to cut through to the bottom). Serve drizzled with sauce, along with some little potatoes and a favourite salad.

Sweet and Sour Meatballs

2 pounds ground beef
2 eggs
1 cup breadcrumbs
1 grated medium onion
½ teaspoon pepper
½ teaspoon garlic powder
½ teaspoon salt

Mix all ingredients together. Shape into meatballs loosely (they'll be more tender). Place on a parchment lined cookie sheet.

Bake at 350 F for 30 minutes. Remove from cookie sheet and place in a casserole dish or small roast pan.

While the meatballs are cooking, prepare the sauce.

In a 2-quart saucepan place:
2 cups brown sugar
2 tablespoons cornstarch
2 cups ketchup
1 cup water
1 cup vinegar
1 teaspoon soya sauce.
Bring to a boil and simmer for 5 minutes.

Pour over meatballs and cover. Bake at 350 F oven for 1 hour.

Sweet and Easy Chili

1 pound ground beef
1 – 28 ounce can herbed tomatoes
1 large can tomato sauce
1 small can crushed pineapple
1 can brown beans in tomato sauce
1 can kidney beans
1 can black beans
1 can kernel corn
5 tablespoons chili powder.

Brown ground beef and place in Dutch oven. Add all the rest of the ingredients. Bring to a bubble and then simmer for 15 minutes. Quick and easy and delicious. Serve with corn bread or biscuits.

Lasagna

Cook 2 pounds of ground beef with 1 large, grated onion, and 5 cloves minced garlic. Drain excess fat. Place in Dutch oven and add two 16-ounce cans herbed diced tomatoes, two 15-ounce cans tomato sauce, 4 tablespoons parsley flakes, 2 teaspoons white sugar, 2 teaspoons basil, 1 teaspoon salt. Simmer for 15 minutes and set aside.

In a bowl, mix together 2 containers lasagna style cottage cheese (smaller curd) and 2 cups parmesan cheese. Set aside.

Grate three–454-gram packs mozzarella cheese and set aside.

Have 2 boxes of oven-ready lasagna noodles ready. Use a 9x13 inch pan and another smaller pan. Layer in each pan as follows: noodles, sauce, cottage cheese mixture, mozzarella cheese. The cottage cheese is only layered the one time in both pans. Then repeat with noodles, sauce, and mozzarella cheese for 2 more layers, ending of course with the mozzarella cheese. Cover with foil wrap.

Bake at 350 F for 1 hour. Let stand for about 30 minutes to rest. It's a good idea to place a cookie sheet under each pan as it will usually spill over. Great with herb bread.

Teddy's Salt Cod Fish Cakes

(15-18 fishcakes)

You will need:
2 pounds salt cod fillets (cooked as noted above)
2 medium onions chopped fine (minced)
2 eggs
14 medium potatoes (boiled, cooled, peeled, and diced)

Boil the 14 medium sized potatoes with the peels left on. Let them come to room temperature and peel once they are completely cool.

Cover the cod in water, and bring to a boil, then drain immediately. If the cod is really salty, repeat by putting cold water on it to cover and bring JUST to a boil and then drain and set aside (the cod is cooked at the first boil but it won't harm it to bring to a boil the second time).

In a very large bowl, put the potatoes, minced onions, eggs, and cod. Mash really well and add pepper to taste. (Or, instead of pepper, try garlic pepper).

Form into fish cakes. Have your frying pan heated up with a little canola oil (just surface oil) and you will have to add a little more oil as you go along until you've cooked all the fish cakes. Just brown them nicely on both sides – all the ingredients are already cooked anyway (except the eggs which cook up quickly) – and just have them nicely browned.

Who is Teddy? He is one of our best friends and when there is a fish cake and beans supper at the local church, he make ALL the fish cakes. They're so good!

Homemade Beans

There are two ways to bake these beans – the long way – in a 250 F degree oven for about 7 hours, OR, in an old-style manual pressure cooker on top of the stove.

Place 1 bag of white pea beans (454g) in a Dutch oven and cover well with water and leave on counter overnight.

In the morning, drain the beans and add 5 cups cold water. Put a cover on the pot and bring to a boil and once boiling, reduce heat and simmer for 30 minutes. Drain the beans and set aside in a large bowl.

Line the bottom of your Dutch oven or casserole dish (or pressure cooker) with an onion sliced in rings.

In a small bowl prepare the following:
½ tablespoon salt
2 teaspoons cider vinegar
1 tablespoon brown sugar
½ teaspoon prepared mustard
¼ cup fancy molasses
¾ cup ketchup
pepper

Mix this up and add to the beans and stir well. Pour the beans on top of the onions in the casserole/Dutch oven or pressure cooker. Cut up ¼ pound of raw bacon (optional but good) and place over the top of the beans. Add water until it comes above the beans. Cover with a lid.

Bake at 250 F for 6½ hours. You may want to add a little water when you check every now and then but usually it is okay.

So good with fish cakes and some hot biscuits or porridge brown bread.

Pressure Cooker Method: Follow the method as above and put the cover on the pressure cooker. Place on burner on high and when the rocker valve on top of the pressure cooker starts to rock, turn heat to medium low and set timer for 35 minutes and once finished, place in sink and let cold tap water run over the cover until the auto lock releases the cover.

Stuffed Pasta Shells

1-box of oven-ready* fillable pasta (jumbo pasta shells/cannelloni/manicotti)
1-500 gram container cottage cheese/or ricotta
1 cup grated parmesan cheese
1 egg
2 cloves garlic, minced
1 tablespoon fresh parsley, chopped
½ cup fresh basil, chopped
½ teaspoon salt
½ teaspoon ground pepper
1 -645ml jar of your favourite marinara/pasta sauce
2 cups grated mozzarella cheese

*If not using oven-ready pasta, cook according to the instructions on the package minus 3 minutes less than the cooking time suggested for pasta *al dente*. Drain and rinse with cool water and set aside.

If using large curd cottage cheese, mix with beater or use a fork to mince up the curd. Then using either the mashed cottage cheese OR the ricotta, add the parmesan cheese, egg, garlic, parsley, basil, salt and pepper and mix really well. (You can make this your own by adding some chopped spinach, some cooked and crumbled sausage, or cooked ground beef.)

Spray a 9x13 inch pan with cooking spray. Pour ½ the pasta sauce in the pan. Fill a plastic bag with the cheese mixture and pipe into the pasta shells and place in the pan. Pour the rest of the pasta sauce over the filled shells and sprinkle with the mozzarella.

Bake at 350 F for 25 minutes. Enjoy.

BREAD

Porridge Brown Bread

Make porridge as follows:
3 cups water and 1 teaspoon salt – bring to boil and add 1 1/3 cup rolled oats. Bring to an immediate boil and simmer for 5 minutes. Pour into a large glass bowl to cool to lukewarm, about 45 minutes. (Cover so that no skin forms on porridge.)

Yeast:
In a small bowl put 1 cup of lukewarm water and dissolve 1 ½ teaspoons white sugar and add 1½ tablespoon active dry yeast. Put in warm spot for 10 minutes.

The rest:
In large bowl put the lukewarm porridge, ½ cup brown sugar, ½ cup
molasses, ¾ cup vegetable oil, 1 teaspoon salt. Mix well and add the yeast.

Place 7 cups all-purpose flour in a separate bowl and add 1 cup at a time. After 5 cups have been added, pour the rest of the flour on counter and push aside and put the dough on the floured board. Keep adding the flour to the dough until all the flour is used kneading while adding the flour. Prepare a large bowl by greasing with oil and place the dough in it. Cover top with plastic wrap and set aside for 1 hour and 30 minutes.

Punch down.

Divide into three even pieces and make a loaf out of each one (or make into rolls). Let rise for 1 hour in the pans.

Place in 325 F oven and bake the loaves for 45 minutes (or if made into rolls – bake for 30 minutes). When loaves or buns are done – brush with butter if desired – this makes a softer crust. If you like a harder crust, don't brush with butter.

Multi-Grain Bread

NB. Best to read recipe through to the end before beginning.

In a large mixing bowl:
1 cup multi-grain cereal (5 or 7 grain – get at bulk food store)
Pour over the cereal – 4 cups of boiling water
Stir and let stand for about 25 minutes until lukewarm (110-115 degrees is optimum) before adding yeast.

In a small bowl:
1 cup lukewarm water
1 teaspoon sugar
Mix well and add 4 ½ teaspoons active dry yeast. Let it stand for 10 minutes – don't add it to the cereal mixture until it has reached lukewarm temperature or it will kill the yeast.

(If using instant yeast – no need to do the above. Just add yeast directly into the lukewarm cereal and add the 1 cup of lukewarm water and the teaspoon of sugar as well – since will be missing that liquid if not using active dry yeast.)

In another bowl measure out the following:
9 cups all-purpose flour. Set aside.

In grain mix which is lukewarm – add 2 tablespoons canola, vegetable or olive oil; 2 tablespoons brown sugar; 2 tablespoons molasses; and 3 teaspoons table salt. Stir well and add the yeast mixture.

Slowly start adding the flour 2 cups at a time. Mix well and keep adding the flour until it's more difficult to mix. Turn the dough out onto a floured surface and keep kneading the bread until flour is all incorporated.

Cover loosely with plastic wrap and let it rest on the counter for 15 minutes.

Remove plastic wrap – and knead for another 5 minutes. Put in a greased bowl and cover with plastic wrap (loosely) and let it rise for 1 hour.

When dough has raised for the hour – remove from pan onto a lightly floured surface. If making into loaves, grease three 9x5 inch loaf pans.
Cut the dough into 3 equal pieces and form into a loaf and lay into the seeded loaf pans. Let raise for 45 minutes.

Bake in a preheated 400 F oven for about 45 minutes.

Check at about the 20-minute mark and if bread is brown enough on the top, drape some foil over the tops and continue to bake for the remaining 25 minutes.

Always preheat your oven before you start baking.

White Bread/Rolls

Put 2 cups of milk in a pot and let it scald. (The milk will get very hot and steamy and little bubbles form around the edge but DOES NOT come to a boil.)

Meanwhile, in a large bowl, add ¼ cup white sugar, 4 teaspoons salt, ¼ cup shortening (cubed into small pieces), and 1 cup of hottest tap water. Mix well.

Pour scalded milk over the water mixture and continue to squash any bits of shortening.

In a 2-cup measuring cup (or any bowl that will hold about 2 cups) put 1 cup of lukewarm water and dissolve 2 teaspoons sugar in the water. Sprinkle 5 teaspoons of traditional active dry yeast* and let stand for 10 minutes.

If not using active-dry yeast, use instant yeast, rapid yeast, bread machine yeast if necessary. Just remember to sprinkle the yeast in the flour but the 1 cup of lukewarm water and the 2 teaspoons of sugar that would have used with the traditional active dry yeast must be replaced so add that to the hot milk mixture.

Once the 10 minutes has passed for raising yeast – make sure shortening mixture is lukewarm. If it is, mix yeast mixture with a fork and then add to the shortening mixture.

Measure out flour into TWO BOWLS as follows:
In Bowl # 1:
5 cups all-purpose flour (and into this flour sprinkle the other kind of yeast (if NOT using the kind dissolved in water) and mix it up.

In Bowl # 2:
Put an additional 5 cups of all-purpose flour and set aside. In the large bowl that has yeast mixture – add Bowl # 1 all at once and with a nice big wooden spoon stir it really, really well until any lumps of flour are incorporated.

Now, from Bowl # 2 – sprinkle in about HALF of that flour and mix well until it has become difficult to mix. Pour the rest of the flour on the work surface (all this flour will be used while kneading). Place dough onto the work surface. Start sprinkling the flour over this surface and push it into the dough with hands – fold the dough over – and if sticky, sprinkle a little more flour. Continue like this until the dough is beginning to come into a dough ball. Fold over the dough and with the heels of your hands – push down and forward. Keep folding over the dough and kneading with the heels of your hands until all the flour is completely used up. This whole process will take about 6 minutes from the time the dough is placed on the work surface until all the flour is incorporated.

Clean out the large bowl and add about a teaspoon of vegetable oil and spread around the whole surface. Place the dough into the bowl and push down in the bowl. Place the bowl on top of a folded towel and loosely cover the bowl with plastic wrap and set it into a nice warm spot (some people place it in the oven with the oven light on). Let it rise for 1½ hours.

After the dough has risen for the 1½ hours – dump the dough out onto the work surface. This recipe will make 4 loaves of bread. What I usually do is make 2 loaves of bread and a cookie sheet of pan

and place 2 balls into each loaf pan and cover very loosely with plastic wrap and place back on a folded towel in a nice warm place free from any drafts or open windows.

Make the rest of the dough into rolls (make them larger like a hamburger bun for lobster rolls or smaller like dinner rolls – or into a muffin tin). Let the bread and the rolls rise for 1¼ hours.

Preheat oven to 400 F. White bread needs a hot oven. Carefully and gently remove the plastic wrap from the bread and the rolls. (If pulled off too quickly – the bread may fall). Place the loaves of bread and the pan of rolls all together into the oven. Set the timer for 20-22 minutes and take the rolls out at that time. Spread out the bread in the oven and let them continue to bake for another 10 minutes.

Immediately remove the rolls from the cookie sheet and place on a cooling rack and brush with butter.

Remove the bread from the oven when 30 minutes is up – remove one loaf from the pan and tap on the bottom – if it sounds hollow – it's done nicely. A thermometer inserted into the loaf of bread is the best way to know if it's completely cooked – 190 F is ideal). Remove both loaves from the pans and place on a cooling rack and brush with some butter. It is best to not cut into the bread until at room temperature.

rolls. Cut the dough exactly in half and set aside (for the rolls), and the other half - cut in 2 – and then in 2 again – so that you have 4 balls of dough to make into bread and a large piece of dough to make into rolls.

Prepare bread pans with a little spray of cooking spray and drape a piece of parchment paper across the bread pan so that the sides drape over – or simply just grease the pan with butter or shortening. Form each piece of dough into a smooth ball

Raisin Bread

In a one-quart pot, put 2 cups raisins* and 1 cup water. Cook on medium high heat until the mixture starts bubbling around the edges, then lower the heat a bit and simmer for 5 minutes. Remove from heat and set aside.

In a bowl put 1½ cups warm water and 1 teaspoon sugar and mix well. Add 1 ½ tablespoons active dry yeast. ** Set timer for 10 minutes.

In largest mixing bowl: ***
whisk 1 egg and add:
2 cups warm water
1 cup milk (1% or 2% or whole milk)
½ cup molasses
2 teaspoons salt
2 tablespoons melted shortening or salted butter (40 seconds or so in microwave)

Add the raisin/water mixture and mix. Make sure the batter is tepid and not too warm.

When yeast has raised for 10 minutes, add to the tepid mixture.

In another bowl, measure out 10 cups all-purpose flour. Sometimes it's a good idea to place a sieve over empty bowl and put the flour into the sieve.

Take largest mixing bowl that has the molasses mixture in it:
Add 2 cups flour and mix – best to use a good wooden spoon.
Add another 2 cups flour and mix well.
Continue adding the flour 2 cups at a time until all 10 cups are mixed in.

On working surface, measure out an additional 2 cups of flour to the side and take some and spread it out on work surface. Put dough on floured surface and sprinkle some flour over the top and using your fingers, push deep into the dough incorporating the flour until able to fold over the dough and it is not as sticky. At this point, it is ready to knead!

Knead the dough, adding and sprinkling flour over and underneath until all the 2 additional cups of flour are used up.

Prepare the largest bowl by putting almost one tablespoon of oil and spread it all around the bowl. Place the dough in the bowl and then turn the dough upside down so that there is oil all over it.

Very, very loosely lay a couple of lengths of plastic wrap over the dough and place the bowl on a doubled-up tea towel, so that it stays warm. Some people put their dough in the oven and just turn the light on in the oven and the light gives off enough warmth to keep the bread safe and sound and also free from drafts from an open door.

Set timer for 1 ½ hours, which is enough time for the dough to double in size.

Dump dough upside down on the counter (do not knead) and cut the dough in half and then cut each half in half again so there are four pieces. Fold each of these into a loaf and massage in case there are some air bubbles and put into 4 parchment lined 9 x 5-inch loaf pans. OR make them the old-fashioned way and cut each piece of dough in half once again so that there are 8 pieces and mold each piece into a ball (folding the dough under as it is shaped) and put 2 pieces in each pan (bum bread). Let rise for about about an hour or until about doubled in size.

Preheat oven to 350 F and bake the loaves for 40 minutes**** (see info re instant thermometer below) and remove from the pans immediately. Place on a cooling rack and brush with butter. Don't cut until the bread is at room temperature.

Notes:
* Lexia raisins are sold at both bulk food and health food stores, and are what Cape Breton cooks call "sticky raisins." If neither of these sources are an option, Thompson seedless raisins are a great alternative.

** If using quick rise or bread machine yeast – put this directly into the measured-out flour but add the 1 teaspoon sugar and the 1½ cups water that would have used with the active dry yeast – into the wet ingredients. I cannot guarantee it will come out the same as I've never used anything other than active dry yeast.

*** My bowl is 12 inches in diameter and about 6 inches high and it is perfect for this batch of bread. I believe it is a 32-cup bowl.

**** The BEST thing when making bread is to have a digital thermometer. The ideal internal temperature for baked bread is 190 degrees F. When making this bread recipe, 40 minutes should bring it to 190 F. If left too long in the oven – it will be dry.

Herb Bread

Yeast Mixture:
1 cup warm water
1 teaspoon white sugar
2 ½ teaspoons active dry yeast (or 1 envelope)
Mix and let stand for 10 minutes.

In a large mixing bowl:
1 cup warm milk (30 seconds in microwave)
3 teaspoons salt
1 tablespoon white sugar

Mix well and add:
2 tablespoons melted butter (10-15 seconds in microwave)
1 tablespoon olive oil
2 teaspoon dried basil (or 1 tsp.)
2 teaspoon oregano (or 1 tsp.)
½ to 1 teaspoon garlic powder
(These spices are my choice only. You may want to add your own such as Italian seasoning, onion seasoning, or perhaps some green onions minced.

Mix well and add yeast mixture.

In a separate bowl, measure out 5 cups all-purpose flour (or bread flour if you have it). Add 1 cup at a time until you've added about 4 cups. Use some of the remaining flour to sprinkle on your work surface. Keep adding flour until the dough is no longer sticky and knead for 2-3 minutes.

Put about 1 teaspoon olive oil in a bowl and spread it around and put the dough in the bowl (getting oil on all the dough). Cover loosely with plastic wrap and set aside for 45 minutes.

Place dough on work surface and divide into 3 even pieces (or just leave it whole and shape into a free form loaf and place on a parchment lined cookie sheet). If divided into 3 pieces – roll each piece into a long piece about 1-2 inches thick and about 14 inches in length.

Place these 3 pieces lengthwise on the parchment lined cookie sheet. Braid the bread from top to bottom. Tuck in the dough edges at the top and the bottom.

Whisk 1 egg and then brush this with a pastry brush on top of the braid and lightly sprinkle top with kosher salt (just a tiny bit and this is optional). Let rise for 15 minutes.

Bake at 400 F for 25-30 minutes. Cool slightly before slicing.

Tea Biscuits

4 cups all-purpose flour
6 teaspoons baking powder
2 teaspoons salt
2 tablespoons white sugar
Mix well with your hands

Add:
½ cup shortening
Mix well with hands until mealy.

Make a well and add:
2 cups milk (see note below)

Incorporate the milk and dry ingredients with a fork until blended. Place on floured surface and bring dough together with hands – knead lightly until the dough forms into a ball.

With a rolling pin, roll out lightly until dough is about 1 inch thick. Cut with a 2- or 3-inch cookie cutter and place on a parchment paper lined cookie sheet (or stoneware pan).

Bake at 425 F oven for about 18 minutes. To test if done: choose a biscuit from the centre and lift out to see if bottom is lightly browned.

Note:
You can replace the milk with an equal amount of buttermilk, or cream, or don't be afraid to use up your sour cream and top it up with milk to make the 2 cups.

Cinnamon Rolls

In a large bowl, place the following ingredients and mix together with your hands:
4 cups all-purpose flour
6 teaspoons baking powder
2 teaspoons salt
2 heaping tablespoons white sugar

Add ½ cup shortening or salted butter (at room temperature) and blend it into the flour with hands, until crumbly. Make a well in centre and add 2 cups of milk. With a fork – scrape all the flour into the milk and combine until all the flour is absorbed and the dough nicely combined. Sprinkle a little flour on work surface and form the dough into a ball and place on the floured surface.

Sprinkle a bit of flour on the dough and on rolling pin and roll out until about ½ inch thickness. Use butter or soft margarine and spread some all over the surface of the rolled- out dough – just like spreading peanut butter on the surface of a slice of bread. Now sprinkle with brown sugar – probably more than a cup – maybe a cup and a half until it is spread out over the entire surface, right to the edges. Now sprinkle cinnamon over the complete surface – don't be shy. Roll up the dough like a jelly roll from the longest side.

With a serrated bread knife cut off both ends of the roll (these pieces can be baked later). Cut into slices about ¾ inch thick and place on the cookie sheet. I use a stoneware 9x13-inch pan, as I find the buns scorch easily in a metal pan. Perhaps use a lower temperature if using a metal pan or even double up your metal pans and this will help the bottom from scorching. Makes about 15 cinnamon rolls.

Bake at 425 F for 18 minutes.

While the buns are baking, make the frosting/ glaze:

Mix together: 3 tablespoons soft salted butter or margarine; 2 teaspoons vanilla, about 2 cups icing sugar, and a little bit of milk – stir and if too thick add a bit more milk until consistency is similar to peanut butter.

Spread over warm cinnamon rolls. Delicious!

Always wash your hands before you bake.

Bonnach

3 cups all-purpose flour (sifted)
1 cup whole wheat flour *
6 teaspoons baking powder
3 teaspoons white sugar
1 teaspoon salt
Mix well and set aside.

In a small bowl:
½ cup vegetable or canola oil
2 cups milk

(Or instead of the oil, add ½ cup shortening or salted butter or lard into flour mixture – then add 2 cups milk)

Pour oil and milk mixture into flour mixture and mix well together just like the method for tea biscuits.

Put out on floured surface and have a little flour on the side to add as needed. Knead a little bit and turn over so that smoothest side is up. Sprinkle a little flour on cookie sheet (or a stoneware or cast-iron frying pan about 10" in diameter) and lay dough in the pan. Score the top of the dough into serving size pieces.

Place in 375 F oven for about 40 minutes. When cooked, remove from pan and place on cooling rack. Serve warm with lots of butter and pour some molasses on top and serve with a good hot cup of tea.

*Can use only all-purpose flour if that's the preference – so 4 cups all-purpose flour in total and omit the 1 cup of whole wheat flour.

Cape Breton Oatcakes

1 cup salted butter (or ½ cup margarine and ½ cup shortening)
½ cup white sugar
1 ½ cups rolled oats (minute or quick)
1 ½ cups all-purpose flour
½ teaspoon salt

Mix together with hands or with a pastry blender. When the mixture is well combined and crumbly, add ½ teaspoon baking soda dissolved in 2 tablespoons of hot tap water. Sprinkle over the dough and using a fork, blend it together. Mixture will be wet.

Roll out on a well-floured surface. (Sprinkle a fair bit of flour under and on the dough and on the rolling pin.) Cut into squares and place on a parchment lined cookie sheet.

Place in 425 F oven for 6-9 minutes until the edges are just browning nicely. Store in a tin container. (If stored in a plastic container – they will get soft.)

Currant/Cranberry Scones

Mix together:
4 cups all-purpose flour
2 teaspoons salt
6 teaspoons baking powder
½ cup sugar

Cut in ¾ cup salted butter with a pastry blender and then finish mixing with hands.

Add: 1 cup currants or more (or any other add-ins such as dried cranberries, dried cherries, nuts, etc.)

Mix until coated and then make a well in the centre.

Beat one egg in a 2-cup measuring cup and then fill with milk (or buttermilk) until it comes to 2 cups.

Mix together until dough is combined. Let stand for about a minute. Turn out onto floured surface and gather the dough together, sprinkling with flour as needed, until it is a ball of dough. Cut this ball of dough in half. Working with one ball, roll out on floured surface until about 1 inch thick (diameter will be about 7 inches). Carefully slice down the centre and then in half again – and then diagonally until there are 8 triangles.

Place the 8 triangles on a stoneware pan OR a parchment lined cookie sheet.

Bake at 425 F for about 16-18 minutes. Roll out the second ball like the first one – and place on the pan once the first batch is baked. The second pan usually take about 2 minutes less baking time – watch carefully.

Serve warm with butter and a good, hot cup of tea.

Variation: Brush the tops of the uncooked scones with milk or cream and add a few thinly sliced almonds on top as a garnish – delicious! Or, once cooled, add a thin drizzle of frosting.

Store oatcakes
in a tin
can container.

Blueberry Lemon Scones with Lemon Curd

Zest and sugar
Measure 1/2 cup sugar and 1 tsp. or more of lemon zest (the rest of the zest from the lemon plus the juice will go in the glaze). Mix the sugar and zest together in a small bowl and set this aside.

Dry Ingredients
Mix the following together in a large bowl: 2 cups all-purpose flour, 1 Tbsp baking powder, 1/2 tsp salt, and then add the sugar/zest and mix well.

Fat
Add 1/2 cup butter (cold or room temperature) to the dry ingredients. If using cold butter, cut in with pastry blender. If using room temperature butter, use your hands and mix up until crumbly. Make a well.

In a bowl, whisk together 1 egg and ½ cup whipping cream and pour into the flour/butter mixture. Mix until dough comes together. Gently, gently pour in 1 cup of fresh blueberries and use your hands to form the dough together without squashing the blueberries. (If you only have frozen blueberries – pour the frozen blueberries into a bowl and lightly dust with flour to try and keep them from bleeding into the dough).

On a floured surface, turn out the dough and pat into a 1-inch-thick circle, about 10 inches in diameter. Cut the dough into eight equal triangles. Carefully place each scone on your baking sheet and brush with additional heavy cream. Just a little bit gives the scones a nice golden colour.

Bake at 400 F for 18-20 minutes or until scones are golden brown on top.

Glaze (optional):
The juice and finely grated rind of one medium/large lemon (will yield 1 tsp to 1 tbsp of grated rind) 1 cup powdered (icing) sugar. Mix together lemon juice, powdered sugar, and zest. Once combined, drizzle the glaze over the cooled scone. Allow the glaze to set before serving.

Serve each scone (glazed or not) with a few tablespoons of the lemon curd and you can add a dollop of whipped cream if you like. Add to that a hot cup of tea in a fancy cup and saucer – take a sip (but make sure you hold your little finger out a bit – there now – just perfect!!). That's good! Now put your feet up and begin reading a Lesley Crewe classic! Enjoy!

Lemon Curd
Before you start, measure out 4 tablespoons of butter and then cut the butter into smaller pieces – set this aside. Prep all the ingredients before you start putting together.

1 large egg and 3 large egg yolks (remove all the chalazae** by using the shell).
½ cup sugar
Juice and zest of 1 lemon (will yield 1 tsp to 1 tablespoon zest and about 1/4 cup of juice
Dash of salt (if using unsalted butter)

In a saucepan, whisk together the whole egg, the egg yolks, sugar, lemon zest, lemon juice, and salt (if using). Bring to a simmer over medium heat, whisking constantly. Continue cooking until mixture is thickened, about 2 ½ to 3 minutes.

Remove from heat. Make sure there are no bits of the chalaza in the mixture and remove with a spoon if you see any (it will be very white). Or, if you want to be sure, put through a fine sieve in a small bowl. Add in the butter, whisking a little piece at a time. Don't add the next piece until the first has melted into the hot lemon. Press plastic wrap directly onto the surface of the lemon curd and refrigerate until cold. Chill before serving. Yield: 1 cup of lemon curd. So lemony and delicious.

*Chalazae: plural, pronounced ka-<u>laze</u>-eye; chalaza: singular, pronounced ka-<u>laze</u>-ah.

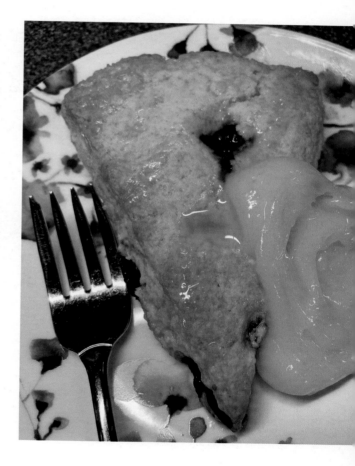

Coffee/Tea Cake

Main Bowl:
1/3 cup soft salted butter or margarine
¾ cup white sugar
Mix well.
Add 1 egg and 1 teaspoon vanilla

Bowl # 2:
Dry Ingredients:
1 ½ cup all-purpose flour
1 ½ teaspoons baking powder
¼ teaspoon salt

Wet Ingredients:
¾ cup milk (or plain yogurt or sour cream)
Using main bowl, stir in about a third of dry ingredients
alternately with milk (or yogurt or sour cream) until all
the ingredients are used.

Bowl # 3 (Topping):
1 cup crushed soda crackers (about 20 crackers)
½ cup chopped walnuts (optional)
½ cup brown sugar
1 teaspoon cinnamon (or two)
1/3 cup melted salted butter or margarine

Pour batter from main bowl into an 8x8-inch pan
(greased or lined with parchment paper) and sprinkle
with topping from Bowl 3. Gently press down.

Bake at 350 F for about 40 minutes. Check with cake
tester in the middle.

Let cool for about 10-15 minutes and enjoy warm with a
good cup of tea!

Amp it up by adding a drizzle of frosting that is quite
thin (try the frosting recipe included in the shortbread
cookie recipe but add more milk (and perhaps just half
that recipe) OR add a drizzle of Mama's Caramel Sauce,
see page 156.

Mabou/An Dròchaid

Mabou is the place where I was born and raised until I married in 1971 and moved to Port Hood for the next fifty years. I love Port Hood, but part of my heart remains in the hills of Mabou.

While Mabou shares many aspects of other small rural communities in Cape Breton, it is the rugged beauty, agriculture, and strong Gaelic cultural ties that set it apart. Mabou itself is actually made up of many Mabous - Little Mabou, Southwest Mabou, West Mabou, Mabou Harbour, Mabou Ridge, Mabou Coal Mines and Northeast Mabou. You will find a high school with a performing arts stage, church, The Gaelic College campus, arena, museum, small businesses, walking trails, a farmer's market and some beautiful beaches too. Mabou is also home to large numbers of musicians, dancers, singers, and Gaelic speakers. It is the place to be if you wish to be immersed in the culture.

There is a quiet yet solid strength in the people of Mabou. I wasn't just raised by my family, but I was raised by this community, and shaped by the people there. There is attention paid to how one

should live a life: to be honest, to be proud of who you are but also to be humble, to never forget your Gaelic roots, to be respectful of everyone, especially those who are older than you, and to honour the 'old' ways. To have that instilled in you at a young age makes you responsible for how you live and act the rest of your life. So thank you Mabou – you will always own a piece of my heart.

Food is a constant in everyone's life, but here where I live, it is key for nourishing the mind, body and soul. Getting the first feed of lobster down at Murphy's Pond wharf, sharing vegetables from the garden with a neighbour, enjoying the taste of homemade cheese with a biscuit, picking blueberries for a pie, having a *strùpach* (a good hot cup of tea and treat) at a little cèilidh, bringing baked goods to someone in need or making a tray of sandwiches for a function at the hall - it is just what we do.

The kitchen will always be the central part of any Cape Breton home – it is the place where a comical story is shared, a heart-to-heart with a friend is had, a lively fiddle tune or song is played, a tidy step given (in stepdancing this means dancing neat and close to the floor), or where the heavenly smell of cinnamon rolls comes from the oven and great hospitality will have you coming back for more.

Toffee Apple Dip

Choose a large round platter (12-14 inches in diameter).

Spread 1–250-gram brick of softened cream cheese on the platter (leaving about an inch around the edges).

Spoon caramel spread* over the cream cheese to cover; (*such as apple dip).

Cut up 4 crunchy toffee chocolate bars and sprinkle over the caramel spread.

Wedge some red apples and some green apples. Place them coloured side up around the edge of the round platter – alternating red and green.

Serve!

Get all your ingredients ready BEFORE you start to bake.

Mama's Caramel Sauce

In a 2-quart saucepan, put 2 cups packed brown sugar and 4 tablespoons cornstarch and mix until combined. Add 1 1/3 cups blend cream (or coffee cream) and 1 cup water, ½ cup corn syrup. Bring just to a boil and keep on a simmer for 4 minutes. Add 3 tablespoons salted butter and 2 teaspoons vanilla. Great on ice cream, cakes, desserts – the best sauce ever! Will keep in fridge for up to 2 weeks. Recipe can be cut in half.

Mama's Chocolate Sauce

In a 2-quart saucepan, place 2 cups white sugar, 3½ tablespoons cornstarch – mix well together and stir in ½ cup cocoa powder and ½ teaspoon salt. Add 3 cups boiling water, and bring mixture to a boil, then simmer for 4 minutes. Add ¼ cup salted butter and 1 teaspoon vanilla. Great for ice cream topping, cake topping, or to make chocolate milk. Will keep in fridge for up to 2 weeks. Recipe can be cut in half.

(Opposite) A recipe from Mommy's scrapbook.

Sauce.

3 egg yolks. 2 cup milk. 1/4 cup sugar.
Vanilla & salt.
Beat yolks slightly. heat milk. & add yolks
slowly. & stir until foam disappears. if it
cooks too long it curdles. Cool & serve.

Carmel Pudding.

2 cups milk scalded.
carmelize 1/2 cup white sugar in frying
pan until it boils gently. When milk
is hot into the melted sugar. Beat 2
eggs in a large bowl & pour hot mixture
into them. Pour into a baking dish &
bake 1/2 hr at 350 degrees. serve with cream

Sauce for Pudding.

1/2 cup butter, 1/2 cup brown sugar.
1 egg yolk, 1 tsp vanilla, 1/2 tsp nutmeg, 1/2 cup water.
Cream butter & sugar. Melt over double-boiler
until it liquids. add beaten yolks & water.
Stir until it thickens, add flavouring. Serve.
Brandy may be added to the above instead of water.

Sabayon Sauce.

Grated rind of 1/2 lemon & juice.
1/4 cup sherry, 1/2 cup sugar. 2 eggs.
Mix lemon, wine & yolks of eggs together
& stir vigorously over fire until it thickens.
Then pour over stiffly beaten egg whites. Serve

Lobster Dip

1 can lobster
1 package softened cream cheese
1 cup mayonnaise

Let the lobster thaw if frozen. Drain lobster and cut into pieces. Mix all ingredients together until blended well.

Vegetable Dip

1 cup mayonnaise
¼ cup chopped green onion
1 clove minced garlic
1 teaspoon Worcestershire sauce

Mix well together and refrigerate. Serve with some fresh cut veggies.

CHEESE/BACON DIP

Two 250-gram packages cream cheese, softened
1 cup mayonnaise
2 cups grated old cheddar
½ package bacon cooked and chopped
1 teaspoon onion powder

Mix together and bake at 350 F for 20 minutes or
hollow out sourdough loaf bread and bake. Just
delicious!!

Cecil's Mustard Chow

Sterilize about 6 (16 ounce) canning jars and lids in boiling water.

12 cucumbers – peel, spoon out seeds, and chop the rest fine.
4 cups onions, chopped fine
½ cup salt
Place all in a large pot, cover, and let stand overnight.

In the morning, drain and rinse well with cold water and set aside.

Use wet measuring cups for liquids.

In another large pot:
Mix 5 cups white sugar with ¾ cup all –purpose flour – mix well.

Add:
4 cups white vinegar
1 teaspoons celery seed
1 teaspoon mustard seed
1 teaspoon dry mustard
1 teaspoon turmeric

Bring this to a boil and let it continue to boil for 2 minutes. Add the prepared vegetables. Return to a boil (this takes a while) and then let the mixture simmer for 10 minutes only. Watch carefully as it scorches easily. Keep stirring often. Bottle immediately. Process in a hot water bath and store in a fridge or cool place.

For more instructions on safe home canning see the Government of Canada website: https://www.canada.ca/en/health-canada/services/general-food-safety-tips/home-canning-safety.html

Cecil's Beets

Cook about 12 medium beets until tender.
While the beets are cooking, sterilize about 6 x
16-ounce jars and lids.

Remove beets when cooked and wait until cool
enough to handle. Slip the peelings off with your
hands. Slice the beets into the hot jars.

In a saucepan, put the following:
4½ cups white vinegar
1½ cups water
2¼ cups brown sugar
Dash of salt

Bring this to a boil and let it simmer for 5 more
minutes.

Pour over beets in the jars until they are covered. If
you run out of the vinegar mixture – just mix up a
little more until you have all the jars filled.

Put covers on snugly over the hot beets. Let cool
at room temperature. You should hear the lids pop
after they seal, and place in fridge or a cool place to
store over the winter.

For more instructions on safe home canning see the
Government of Canada website: https://www.canada.ca/
en/health-canada/services/general-food-safety-tips/home-
canning-safety.html

CRANBERRY SAUCE

1- 12 ounce package fresh cranberries
¾ cup white sugar
¼ cup orange juice
¾ cup water
Orange zest

In medium saucepan, mix water, zest, orange juice, and sugar together. Bring to a boil. Add cranberries. Cover and simmer until the berries burst (about 5 minutes). Remove from heat and mash with a potato masher a little. Cool. Spoon into container. Cover and refrigerate when cool. Sauce will thicken as it cools.

Strawberry Freezer Jam

Follow this recipe EXACTLY so that the jam will gel. You cannot cut back on the sugar. You will need 2 boxes of liquid pectin. (There are two pouches in each box).

1 batch makes about 4 x 1 cup or 240 ml jars.

2 large containers /4lbs of fresh strawberries (This will make 4 batches (16 one-cup jars).

Wash strawberries and dry off with paper towels. Hull strawberries (1 container at a time) and cut in half. Mash with potato masher but still leave some chunks.

Measure out 2 cups mashed strawberries and put into a medium size bowl and add 4 cups white sugar. Mix well and set aside and time for 10 minutes.

Wash the jars and lids with soap and hot water and rinse with hottest water. Place upside down on tea towel along with lids.

When 10 minutes is up on the mashed strawberries, add 2 tablespoons lemon juice and one pouch of the liquid pectin. Stir continually for 3 full minutes. Pour into jars and seal and let stand for 24 hours at room temperature and then put in freezer. When you take the jam out of the freezer and open it, it will last about 2 weeks in the refrigerator.

Easy Cheesy Dip

1- 250- gram block cream cheese (softened to
room temperature)
1-230 gram tub cheddar, softened to room
temperature
½ small onion (grated)
1 splash Worcestershire sauce

Put all ingredients together in a bowl and beat with
an electric beater.

Split the batter and put in 2 small containers
and refrigerate. Serve with your favourite crackers
OR garnish as follows:

Crush walnuts and sprinkle on one of the halves
of the dip and coat all sides and form cheese into
a ball. Refrigerate wrapped in plastic wrap but
remove from refrigerator half hour before serving.

Shape the other half in the shape of a pinecone
and cover with whole almonds to make it look
like a pinecone – garnish with greenery (rosemary
sprigs, fresh parsley, fresh basil leaves, pine tree
sprig) and add a couple of fresh raspberries or
cherry tomatoes.

Invest in a good
thermometer to
check temperature
of baked goods
and meat.

Denise's Salsa

10-14 ripe tomatoes peeled and chopped (par boil for 2 min then skin and cut up)
1-4.5 ounces/125 ml can green chilies.
1 large onion, chopped
1 large red onion, chopped
2 large green peppers, chopped
2 large red peppers, chopped
1-215 gram jar jalapeno peppers
1–5 ounce can tomato paste
¾ cup white vinegar
1 tablespoon pickling salt
¼ cup brown sugar
1 teaspoon paprika
2 teaspoons garlic cloves, minced

Mix all ingredients in a large pot and simmer uncovered for 1 hour, stirring occasionally. Pour into sterilized jars and seal. Makes about six 1 cup jars.

For more instructions on safe home canning see the Government of Canada website: https://www.canada.ca/en/health-canada/services/general-food-safety-tips/home-canning-safety.html

Who is Denise? She is my hair stylist.

A Life Journey

My earliest memory of baking was watching Mama kneading bread in a small room off the kitchen called the 'pantry'. By today's standards this space was minimalistic; there were two or three shelves for dishes, another shelf behind the door for odds and ends, and a cupboard with a latch on it that she called a *snagan* (a Gaelic word pronounced "snack-in").

The cupboard was made of wood that Papa sanded. It had a nail in the middle, and we would turn it to the right so it would keep the cupboard closed. This was where larger items were stored and baking was hidden until you were allowed to eat it. If there was a mess and someone came down the long driveway, we were told to clean up and hide the mess in there.

Making Bread

The bread would have been mixed in a large white enamel basin, trimmed in red. This type of vessel was a staple in many homes throughout rural Cape Breton. That basin also served as a pan to heat milk on the woodstove when making homemade cheese or curds; and as a mixing bowl for other large yield recipes Mama would have prepared to feed our family. When the tasks of cooking and baking were finished, this basin was re-purposed as the dishpan as there was no sink in the pantry. Due to the basin's multipurpose existence, the enamel had worn off in a few places on the bottom. I distinctly remember the sound the cutlery made as it shifted over those worn spots while Mama washed the dishes, and that noise would send shivers up my spine.

My precious parents – Margie and Donald MacDonald.

I was born on a stormy winter day in 1952 to Margie (Mommy) and Donald (Daddy) MacDonald of Mabou. Mommy was a MacDonell from Glengarry near Mabou. My mother had given birth to four other children before me, one of whom died at one month old.

While pregnant with my youngest brother, my mother was diagnosed with cancer. Her declining health made raising five children a great challenge but in Cape Breton, family looks after family. So, while Mommy was sick, Daddy would bring me to Southwest Mabou to stay with my grand-aunt Maggie Ann and her husband John Beaton. I was about a year old the first time I went.

Over the next couple of years, I was back and forth between the two homes until eventually I just stayed in Southwest Mabou. That's what made sense back then. Maggie Ann and John became known to me as Mama and Papa.

Aunt Flora

My younger brother eventually went to another grand-aunt's home in Mabou Harbour, and my three older siblings remained with Daddy. His sister Flora Mae lived in the home, so she helped care for the older children while he was working. My mother contracted tuberculosis following her cancer diagnosis but succumbed to cancer when I was three and a half years old.

My siblings and I ranged in age from two to nine years old at the time of our mother's passing. After the funeral, someone lined us up on the couch and took a picture of us. We were all smiles in that photo as I believe we were not old enough to realize the sadness that engulfed the rest of the house. Our mother was only 37 years old.

Mommy's Scrapbook

My memories of my mother are scarce, but I've always been told that Mommy was a beautiful Gaelic singer and that she also loved to dance. I'm told she was a wonderful baker. Thankfully, she kept a scribbler filled with her most cherished recipes that has just recently been passed on to me.

How I wish I had been able to know her or at least remember more about my mother. I do have vivid memories in which I can recall moments, colours, and other details. I can envision her hand reaching out to me from a bed and in the palm of her hand were two yellow candies.

In another memory Mommy had come to visit me at Mama and Papa's house. Mama was kneading bread in the pantry, and I was running back and forth between Mama and Mommy. I can recall

Mommy's coat being a dark navy blue and that I sat in her lap pointing at and counting the buttons that were covered in the same fabric as her coat. These buttons seemed huge to me.

Mama, who raised me. She was 93 when this photograph was taken. She died two weeks later.

Red Slippers

Another memory I have is of Mama and Papa taking me back home to visit with Mommy and Daddy. I remember walking into the house and seeing my mother standing at the stove. I only see her from the waist down. She was wearing fluffy red slippers on her feet with the backs flattened. I was captivated by them.

My final memory of my mother was at her wake which was held in Mommy and Daddy's house. As Mama held me in her arms, I can remember reaching my hand up under her glasses and wiping her tears away and asking her why she was crying.

As I stood beside my mother's casket, I remember reaching down and touching her clothes. The fabric was white, or off-white and it was silky.

Sadly, I am unable to see her face in any of these memories. I am thankful to have old photographs and I see how I resemble her.

Family Circle

I had an incredibly good life with the Beatons in Southwest Mabou. I was embraced and surrounded by love from Mama and Papa and their six children, and my family circle grew. I was ten years younger than their youngest child, so I guess I was a bit of a welcome novelty. Mama and Papa spoke Gaelic as their first language in their home and passed the language on to their children.

Before Mama was married, she worked in Boston for a wealthy family and she was the dessert lady. She was a fine baker and she took some of those recipes home with her. When she came back to Mabou at the age of 32, she married Papa.

Papa was a fisherman. A quiet, gentle man who believed in always doing the right thing. He never raised his voice and what I remember most about him is how he loved to slurp his tea from a teacup and saucer.

Traditions

Traditional music and dancing seemed to be valued less and less in this era but in our Beaton home, Mama and Papa worked hard at maintaining these valued cultural traditions.

Lively gatherings with music were known as céilidhs and the Beaton home was no stranger to them. Neighbours and family would often come by filling the house with Gaelic songs, Irish songs, Scottish songs, Country songs and of course, fiddlers and stepdancers.

No céilidh was complete without a hot cup of tea (served in a cup and saucer just the way Papa liked it) with biscuits or homemade bread, a slice of homemade cheese, and usually a piece of pie, a square, or a cookie. Food, music and love were shared in abundance and enjoyed by the many visitors that came and went through the doors of the home I was raised in.

Big Dan Cameron

Our ancestors from Scotland brought stepdancing to Cape Breton Island when they settled here, and this tradition was practiced in our home. Learning how to stepdance came naturally to me with guidance from Mama. Her father, Big Dan Cameron, was a noted stepdancer.

My sister Minnie was very talented and, as they say, light on her feet. She was a wonderful teacher and as my older sister she encouraged me to stepdance with her on stage when I was just four. I made my debut at the Mabou Parish Hall.

I remember the crowd's loud cheers and applause at the end of my performance, and it was very overwhelming for me. When I think back to that time, I am not sure if the response to my dancing was because I was a cute little four-year-old or if it was sympathy for a young girl whose mother had recently passed away. I remember feeling very shy as I put my finger in my mouth and I left the stage to find Mama. I crawled into her lap, put my head down and cried.

Hughie and Allan

I clearly recovered from my emotional debut as this was the beginning of a major part of my life. I continued to dance at many concerts with Minnie and eventually on my own. I was even asked to perform on live television programs. I think I was just seven or eight when I first danced on the *Hughie and Allan Show*; a variety show hosted by a well-known comedy duo from the Sydney area and over the years there were many other programs I was a part of. As a Gael, the love of the language, the love of the fiddle and dancing, and the love of the stories that accompanied the culture were rooted deep in my soul.

I attended school from Grade 8 to Grade 12 at Mabou Consolidated School (MCS). It was so big and it was so exciting to attend after being in the smaller St. Joseph's Convent for my earlier schooling.

Cecil and I on our wedding day in 1971.

Students came from around our province of Nova Scotia to attend a wide range of programs aimed at a variety of learners.

Daddy, after working away for many years in the mines, was now the school's custodian, and I was overjoyed at having the chance to see him every day. During my days at MCS I discovered Home Economics, my favourite class of all. We learned to sew and to bake and I immediately felt a real connection.

Sunday Supper

At home I practised what I learned by making cookies and squares for Mama and Papa. I would also make supper on Sunday evenings. My regular menu was sliced ham from that oval can that wound open with the key. I cut myself on that contraption so many times! I would serve them ham with sliced tomatoes, cheese, homemade bread, and tea, followed by cookies or pie. Oh how I loved cooking and baking for them.

When I was in Grade 11 the custodian's broom sat idle in the school hallway at Mabou Consolidated as my father died suddenly at the age of 54. He always made porridge early in the mornings and at that time, only my brother John Donald lived at home. When he came downstairs to go to work, there was no porridge ready and Daddy's truck was still in the driveway. He had suffered a heart attack in the middle of the night. Maybe part of it was from a broken heart. I really don't think he ever got over losing my mother. They were both so young.

Prom Date

I graduated in 1969 and Cecil MacDonald was my date for my Grade 12 prom. I went on to take a job at the Court House in Port Hood as a secretary

Marie - the most wonderful mother-in-law.

with the local school board. I was 17, confident, and couldn't wait to spend my $50 a week earnings ordering something from the Simpson Sears or Eaton's catalogue. Those were the days!

Cecil and I married in 1971 and moved to Port Hood and I absolutely fell in love with my mother-in-law, Marie. She and her husband Willie raised 13 children of which Cecil was the second youngest. She was like my third mother and her influence on me was strong. Any chance I had, I would drop in for a visit.

Homemade Goodies

She would put the teapot on and always had a stash of homemade goodies. Her oatcakes, molasses cookies, biscuits, and homemade bread were the very best I had ever tasted, and I still make those recipes today. She was a humble and wise woman with whom I had many great conversations and I still miss her so much.

Cecil and I had seven children and I was a mother who worked full time. In fact, I stayed with the school board for more than 30 years.

No matter how busy life was with a big family, I never wavered from the task of baking from scratch. I must admit that most days it was done from necessity. Keeping seven children fed was not an easy job. I rose early to bake, mostly because if I did so in the evenings, there would be nothing left come morning!

When I look back, it was the one time of day there was calm. Like the calm before the storm!

As mothers we find ways to survive the struggles. My children simply remember waking to the aroma of fresh baked goods cooling on the counter when they got out of bed, and it is such a happy memory for them; sitting on chairs around the open oven door enjoying the heat that was used to make their goodies.

A Busy Life

Cecil took over the task of grocery shopping and sharing meal preparation as life got busier, but I hung on to the task I loved of making the 'treats.'

During these years, there was a concern that a decline was occurring in our traditions so as a way of earning some extra income as well as helping keep

Me with the girls L-R: Margie, Kelly, Krista, and Tammy.

those traditions alive, I began teaching stepdancing. I taught many nights a week in Port Hood and surrounding communities, and I could barely keep up with the demand for lessons. I taught for more than 30 years.

Stepping Out

In1983 I was asked to travel to Scotland to teach stepdancing at the Barra Feis. For the next 17 years or so, I travelled to many places bringing the Cape Breton style of stepdancing to California, Chicago, Seattle, Utah, the Yukon, back to Scotland many times, and even once, to Denmark.

I made two instructional videos to help people learn how to stepdance in the comfort of their own homes. I no longer stepdance but I often think of that four-year-old girl crying in my Mama's lap. Little did she know how stepdancing would provide such incredible opportunities to travel to so many places throughout the world.

In Mother's Shoes

A powerful moment for me was when I turned 37. I tried to imagine being in my mother's shoes; being so young and facing death. I looked at my seven children and wondered how in the name of God was she able to accept her fate, knowing she would be leaving all her young ones. In the depths of her illness, she had the strength and foresight to pack things away and label them for each child so that we'd have something of hers.

I truly wish I had known my mother, to have been able to talk to her or hear her voice; to be able to hug her and spend time with her dancing or singing or baking. But this wasn't to be.

The 'fam' and me stepdancing at the Broad Cove Concert. L-R:. Mitchell, Krista, Kelly, Gordie, Brennan, Tammy, and MJ (Margie had a sprained ankle so couldn't dance).

Despite the losses, I have enjoyed a rich and beautiful life. Every time my children tell me they made Port Hood Grandma's biscuits or Mabou Grandma's Chocolate Pudding, we remember them. Every time they stepdance or sing on stage or in the living room, I know I have done my duty at passing on the legacy of those who shaped me.

And this brings us to the pandemic.

By now, you all know the story. I baked cinnamon rolls live on Facebook one Sunday as a fun way to stay connected to my kids, and from that *Tunes and Wooden Spoons* was born.

Cecil and the boys L-R: Cecil, Gordie, Mitchell, and Brennan.

A Love Letter to My Grandchildren

Our oldest daughter Tammy was the first to be married and I clearly remember the day she told me that she was expecting a baby. A jolt went through me at the realization that I would be a grandmother. She was due in early June and the days and weeks went by way too slowly for my fancy.

Tammy's birthday was May 27. Getting close to midnight on the eve of her birthday, the phone rang. It was Tammy and she was in labour. She said, "But I don't want this baby to have the same birthday as me. I want this baby to have their own birthday!!!"

That made me laugh and I just told her that she had no control over that. So, on May 27, Brody James Stanley was born and gave his mother the best birthday gift ever. That was back in 1999 and to date, eleven more grandchildren have been born and have filled our lives and hearts with so much love. A dozen blessings for Grandma and Grandpa.

Brody, Ben, Jake, Oliver, Anna, Mary Sarah, Luke, Charlie, Aiden, Iver, Asher, and Rosie, as of this year of 2021, range in age from 1 to 22. There is no better feeling in the world than spending time with them. Hearing "I love you Grandma," or getting a text that says the same thing, or hugs or the little words "I wuv you," or "I wuv you mo," means the world. Nothing can compare the love that they bring.

Being a mother is a huge job, but being a grandmother brings a whole lot of freedom. It's like getting a raise at work — you're putting more cash in your heart's bank account and you don't care how you spend it.

When you say "no" to your child, you say yes to your grandchild without even thinking twice. Just chatting with the older grandchildren and hearing their plans and hopes and dreams and seeing them grow into responsible adults is so amazing to me. The younger ones bring just as much joy when they drop in for a visit and you see them go from crawling to walking to talking to singing — nothing better.

Spending some time with them and baking cookies or cinnamon rolls is always a special time. I can recall some of them believing so much in my baking and saying "Grandma, you have to open a bakery — you could make a million dollars." That unabashed belief that their Grandma was the best ever. How sweet is that?

So, to my grandchildren I want to say thank you. Thank you for loving me with all your hearts, thank you for loving my baking and for baking with me on occasion, thank you for taking the time to visit especially when you live far away, thank you for sharing your schemes and dreams, thank you for being respectful to your moms and dads, thank you for always loving coming home to visit Grandpa and me.Know that I love you with every part of my heart and that I'm here for you whenever you need me. I hope, and I know, that you will all grow up to be the best YOU there is and know that I will always be there in body or spirit to celebrate all the wonderful things that will happen in your life.

Just like little Asher says it "I wuv you mo." Always remember: love one another.

Love from Grandma.

(Above) Grandchildren: Back Row L-R: Aiden, Ben (holding Iver), Luke (holding Charlie), Jake, and Brody. Front Row L-R: Anna, Mary Sarah, and Oliver.

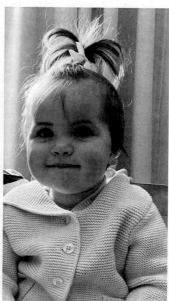

Right: Asher and (Far Right) Rosie

The History of Aprons

I don't think most kids today know what an apron is. The principle use of Mom's or Grandma's apron was to protect the dress underneath because she only had a few. It was also because it was easier to wash aprons than dresses and aprons used less material.

But along with that, an apron served as a potholder for removing hot pans from the oven. It was wonderful for drying children's tears, and on occasion was even used for cleaning out dirty ears. From the chicken coop, the apron was used for carrying eggs, fussy chicks, and sometimes half-hatched eggs to be finished in the warming oven. When company came, those aprons were ideal hiding places for shy kids, and when the weather was cold, she wrapped it around her arms.

Those big old aprons wiped many a perspiring brow, bent over the hot wood stove. Chips and kindling wood were brought into the kitchen in that apron. From the garden, aprons carried all sorts of vegetables. After the peas had been shelled, the aprons carried out the hulls. In the fall, the apron was used to bring in apples that had fallen from the trees. When unexpected company drove down the lane, it was surprising how much furniture that old apron could dust in a matter of seconds. When dinner was ready, she walked out onto the porch, waved her apron, and the menfolk knew it was time to come in from the fields to dinner.

In today's world, people go crazy trying to figure out how many germs are on that apron. I don't think I ever caught anything from that apron but love.

(Adapted from Tina Trivett's poem to her grandmother)

Preserving a Piece of the Scottish Highlands

This is a typical house 'ceilidh' (Gaelic for a visit) held in Mabou at the home of Raymond and Sarabelle Beaton. I'm at the far left, listening to awesome tunes with great people.

Tucked within the valleys of the Cape Breton Highlands, in communities with names like Mabou, Inverness and Port Hood, are spots where Old World Gaelic culture has been nurtured and blossomed. In these places, the old people still speak some Gaelic; they pass it down to their children and grandchildren who keep the language alive. Young people learn to sing songs in Gaelic and to dance to the old strathspeys, reels, and jigs. They still tell the stories and legends their ancestors brought with them from the old country; and gather in kitchens on Saturday nights to play the old tunes on well-worn fiddles and grandfathers' bagpipes, sing songs, and play dusted-off guitars.

My daughter Kelly and I singing at the annual Celtic Colours International Festival, held each fall in Cape Breton.

Family recipes in these communities are passed down through generations with respect and reverence for those who first perfected them, while Gaelic milling frolics and céilidhs still serve as important forms of entertainment. It's a place that has nurtured a long list of international Celtic stars including Natalie MacMaster, the Rankin Family, Ashley MacIsaac, and John Allan Cameron.

Cape Breton Gaelic culture is filled with music, singing, and dancing. In the old days, songs were often set to the rhythms of the farm. Whenever Scottish settlers had an arduous task to perform such as harvesting the fields, milking cows, building a barn, or hand-milling cloth — they had a repertoire of songs to go with the task. And all of them were sung in Gaelic.

Today, Gaelic can still be heard in the valleys that slice through the Mabou Highlands. Like the Acadian French that survives in Chéticamp to the north, and the Mi'kmaq spoken just east of here in Whycocomagh, the language has been preserved thanks to the remoteness of Inverness County and the perseverance of the people who speak it.

At one time Gaelic was the third most common European language in Canada, with large pockets spoken in New Brunswick, Newfoundland, Eastern Ontario and even Quebec. Between 1896 and 1954, Nova Scotia had a Gaelic-speaking premier for all but 11 years. And Alexander MacKenzie, Canada's second prime minister, spoke Gaelic as his first language.

But in the 20th century, efforts to assimilate the Gaelic people took a huge toll on the language. Today Nova Scotia © Cape Breton more specifically — is the only place in North America where Gaelic

still has a foothold. The Highlands around Mabou hang on fiercely to their Gaelic traditions.

Stepdancing at the Judique Community Centre during Celtic Colours International Festival a few years ago.

Every October, when Cape Breton's tree-covered mountains burst into the iridescent reds and yellows of autumn, the island plays host to the Celtic Colours International Festival, a nine-day celebration of the music and culture of Cape Breton. The festival is a pilgrimage for many international performers.

For generations now, Celtic musicians from Scotland and around the world have been making the journey to Cape Breton to learn their own traditional music at the hands of the local masters who have kept it alive.

They also come to visit Colaisde na Gàidhlig, the Gaelic College in St. Ann's, a unique institution founded in 1938 to preserve and perpetuate the Highland Scottish language and culture for future generations. In addition to studying the Gaelic language and traditional music, students at the College can learn Gaelic storytelling, drama, step dance, and history.

Today, Gaelic language and culture is experiencing a resurgence in places around the world where Scottish culture predominates. But in Cape Breton it never really left. And thanks to the tenacious people of the Cape Breton Highlands, the language and culture are here to stay.

Thank you

To these beautiful people for their help:

Bob Martin
Dawn & Margie Beaton
Dr. Robert Strang
John Gillies
Katy Allen
K.C. Beaton
Lesley Crewe
Linden MacIntyre
Natalie MacMaster
Raymond & Sarabelle Beaton
Shelly Campbell
To Margie's friends in Fort McMurray for photo props

Technical and hosting help on the show:

Charlaine Chiasson
Frank MacDonald
Hans Thorhauge Dam
Kelli MacDonald
Laura MacDonald
Michael Nikas Dismatsek
Roderick Morris

To the singers, bakers, authors, poets, and musicians who shared their talents on my show:

Aaron MacDonald
Andrea & Betty Beaton
Ashley LeBlanc
Beolach
Bill & John Pellerine

Bonnie Jean MacDonald
Bradley Murphy
Brennan & Anna, Kelly, Krista, Mitchell
Christine Campbell and daughters Mairinn, Eilidh, and Sèonaid
Dawn & Margie Beaton
Donelda MacDonnell
Eddie Cummings
Glen MacNeil
Jason Price
Jeremy White
Jimmy Inch
Joan MacNeil
Joe MacMaster
Keith MacNeil
Kenneth & Jenny MacKenzie
Lesley Crewe
Lionel & Jessie Margaret LeBlanc
Lisa Cameron and son Finley
Lynn Chisholm
Mac Morin
Mairi Britton
Mamie MacDougall
Mary Beth Carthy
Michelle Deveau
Morgan Toney
Nick Boudreau
Nicole Deveau
Peter MacInnis
Pius MacIsaac
Reg Landry
Rita Rankin
Robert Bouchard
Rodney MacDonald

Sarabelle Beaton & Joan Currie
Sarah MacInnis
Steve MacIntyre
Theresa MacDonell
Troy MacGillivray
Wendy MacIsaac
Wendy Markey MacPhee

To the people who made this book a reality:

Copy Editor Lindy Mechefske
Designer Denis Cunningham
Photographer Margie MacDonald
Photographer Bob Martin (author photo back cover)
Managing Editor Vernon Oickle
Publisher John MacIntyre
Mats Melin from Ireland (Celtic Colours photos)

Index of Recipes

Facebook:
https://www.facebook.com/TunesAndWoodenSpoons

YouTube:
https://www.youtube.com/tunesandwoodenspoons

Website:
www.tunesandwoodenspoons.com